YOU AND YOUR SPOUSE HAVE
DECIDED TO DIVORCE.

THE CAR YOU JUST BOUGHT
TURNS OUT TO BE A LEMON.

YOU ARE HAVING A BILLING DISPUTE WITH A
DEPARTMENT STORE OR CREDIT CARD COMPANY.

In these and many, many other cases,
this book could save you a lot of
time and a lot of money.

STEVEN SARSHIK is a graduate of the University
of Pennsylvania and New York University School of
Law. He was Special Counsel to the New York City
Department of Consumer Affairs in the early 70s. He
now has his own legal practice in New York City.

WALTER SZYKITKA is a free-lance writer living
and working in New York City. He has been at
various times a truck driver, waiter, secretary, taxi
driver, minister, tour conductor, travel agent and
door-to-door salesman. He edited and compiled
Public Works: A Handbook for Self-Reliant Living,
and *How to Be Your Own Boss*, available
in a Plume edition.

Without A Lawyer

by

Steven Sarshik
and Walter Szykitka

A PLUME BOOK
NEW AMERICAN LIBRARY
TIMES MIRROR
NEW YORK, LONDON AND SCARBOROUGH, ONTARIO

NAL BOOKS ARE ALSO AVAILABLE AT DISCOUNTS IN BULK QUANTITY FOR INDUSTRIAL OR SALES-PROMOTIONAL USE. FOR DETAILS, WRITE TO PREMIUM MARKETING DIVISION, NEW AMERICAN LIBRARY, INC., 1633 BROADWAY, NEW YORK, NEW YORK 10019

Copyright © 1980 by Steven Sarshik and Walter Szykitka

Legal forms reprinted with the permission of and available from Julius Blumberg, Inc., New York, New York 10013.

PLUME TRADEMARK REG. U.S. PAT. OFF. AND FOREIGN COUNTRIES
REGISTERED TRADEMARK—MARCA REGISTRADA
HECHO EN WESTFORD, MASS., U.S.A.

SIGNET, SIGNET CLASSICS, MENTOR, PLUME, MERIDIAN AND NAL BOOKS are published *in the United States* by The New American Library, Inc., 1633 Broadway, New York, New York 10019, *in Canada* by The New American Library of Canada Limited, 81 Mack Avenue, Scarborough, Ontario M1L 1M8, *in the United Kingdom* by The New English Library Limited, Barnard's Inn, Holborn, London, EC1N 2JR, England

Library of Congress Cataloging in Publication Data

Sarshik, Steven.
 Without a lawyer.

 (A Plume book)
 1. Law—United States—Popular works.
I. Szykitka, Walter, joint author.   II. Title.
KF387.S25   349.73   79-27563
ISBN 0-452-25226-1

First Printing, March, 1980

2   3   4   5   6   7   8   9   10

PRINTED IN THE UNITED STATES OF AMERICA

To Elaine and Barbara

Acknowledgment

We wish to express our deep appreciation to the following attorneys who provided us with useful information and who generously gave their time to help us unravel complicated points of law: Doug Ackerman, Guy Blynn, Mort Dicker, Judy Garson, Greg Hiestand, Mary Hilgeman, Susan Ingram, and Ephraim Liebowitz.

Contents

Contents

Introduction

A few years ago, *The New York Times* printed a story about a woman who obtained her own divorce without a lawyer. The woman had purchased a how-to-do-it paperback and followed the instructions. When she arrived in court, the woman said, "Three lawyers were there with their clients. They all happened to be men. When they heard that I didn't have a lawyer, they were appalled. They said, 'Good luck, lady, you'll never get your divorce.' I felt defeated, and I thought, well, I probably won't get it, but I'm not giving up. Then—I couldn't believe it—all three divorces were denied because one paper or another was missing." The woman who was doing it herself, however, had all the proper forms, and her application for a divorce was granted in a few minutes.

In recent years, more and more people have found it advantageous to represent themselves in uncontested divorce proceedings. This has been part of the growing do-it-yourself movement which has spread throughout the country.

The purpose of this book is to provide a guide for people who want to handle their own legal problems without a lawyer. In the following chapters you will find information about contracts, leases, corporations, consumer credit, divorce, bankruptcy, and many other areas of the law. This information is presented not in textbook form, but in everyday language that you can understand. To explain certain points, we have included examples and actual case histories, although in some instances the names have been changed. In some sections of the book, we have also included letters and sample forms. Obviously, these forms cannot cover every conceivable set of circumstances, but in many cases they can be adapted to your own use.

It is now apparent that there are some legal transactions which do not require a lawyer. As a practical matter, consumers often read and approve their own contracts without the help of a lawyer. They do so despite the fact that the amounts involved in these contracts are often substantial. The purchase price of a new automobile is over $5,000 and, if inflationary trends continue, will soon be over $10,000. But most people sign these contracts without taking them to a lawyer for review. That is why it is imperative that they have some information about cancellation rights, warranties, and Truth-in-Lending provisions.

A similar point can be made about apartment leases. Few people have the time or the money to have an attorney review the terms of a new lease, and most tenants are forced to act as their own legal counsel. The chapter on leases explains how to negotiate with your landlord, how to protect yourself if the landlord fails to provide essential services, and how to arrange to sublet your apartment.

The book also provides information about forming a corporation and filing a petition for bankruptcy—tasks which have traditionally been performed by lawyers. Some candid observers have pointed out that the "legal work" in these areas consists primarily of filling out a series of forms. In fact, in some law offices which handle a heavy volume of business, the forms are filled out by special assistants called "paralegals," or by secretaries. So it seems clear that in many cases an individual can form a corporation or file a petition for bankruptcy without spending several hundred dollars in legal fees.

In preparing the material for this book, we have decided not to include information on criminal law. A person who is indicted or charged with a criminal offense should always retain an attorney to represent him. If you are tempted to act on your own behalf and represent yourself in a criminal proceeding, remember that it will be difficult to keep up with your new vocation as an advocate while you are busy making license plates in prison.

There is no information presented in this book on buying a house. According to recent statistics, the average price of a new house is now more than $70,000. For many people the purchase of a new home will represent the largest investment they will ever decide to make. Since so much money is involved in the purchase of a house, and since the laws concerning the transfer of real property differ from state to state, we recommend that you retain an attorney before buying a house.

Finally, there is no information presented in this book about writing your own will. There are two reasons for this. First, the laws concerning wills and estates differ in each jurisdiction. It would probably be impossible to prepare a complete and accurate guide that would be applicable in every situation and in every state. Second, the cost of hiring a lawyer to prepare a will is not great. Some lawyers charge less than $100 to prepare a "simple will." So all things considered, it pays to have an attorney draw up your will.

It should be pointed out that it is not a good idea to try to represent yourself in contested matters in court. The one important exception to this rule, of course, is Small Claims Court. This is a special court set up in many cities to hear cases involving small sums of money. It is the perfect place to file a suit against a dry cleaner who ruins your coat or a landlord who refuses to return a security deposit. Because the subject is so important, there is a separate chapter devoted to procedures in Small Claims Court. At the end of the chapter there is a chart which contains information about Small Claims operations in forty major cities.

Every reasonable effort has been made to make this book complete and accurate. Readers should be aware, however, that it is not possible in a book of this nature to delve into complicated or minute points of law or to explain the statutes and regulations which have been enacted in each one of the fifty states. Throughout this book, we have presented general legal principles applicable in most cases and have tried to indicate important exceptions where possible.

As you read this book, keep in mind that the law is constantly changing. This book focuses on the law in effect at this time, and it is simply not possible to anticipate all of the changes or modifications which may take place in the future.

In the final pages there is a glossary which contains definitions of many of the words used in this book. It also includes many legal terms which you have probably heard on television or read in the newspaper. The definitions presented in the glossary are not intended to be technical, but are intended to give you a simple "common-sense" understanding of the words. The glossary may even be of some help to you if you retain a lawyer to represent you in a court proceeding. Lawyers sometimes speak in technical jargon which is not readily understandable to the layperson. If your lawyer tells you that he is going "to put the case on the calendar as soon as he completes the interrogatories and schedules a deposition," you can use the glossary to translate his statement into words that you can understand.

Nothing in this book is intended as a criticism or disparagement of lawyers. Most lawyers are competent, industrious people who do excellent work for their clients. The average person, however, is not always able to obtain the type of help that he needs. Most lawyers and law firms in large urban areas handle big clients or small clients with big problems. There are few—very few—attorneys in private practice who devote a substantial part of their time to helping individuals with their consumer contracts, leases, and credit obligations. The fact remains that most people have to confront these problems without a lawyer. We hope that this book will give them the information and encouragement that they need.

Contracts

The popular notion is that all contracts are formalized legal documents. But this is simply not the case. When you go to the supermarket, you make a contract with the market to pay for the items you present at the checkout counter. When you go to a service station, you make a contract to buy gasoline for the price indicated on the pump. When you order home delivery of the newspaper, you make a contract to pay for the papers delivered to your home. All such transactions—without benefit of either formal documents or lawyers—involve the making of contracts.

What Is a Contract?

The law, in its stilted fashion, defines a contract as "a promise or a set of promises for the breach of which the law gives a remedy, or the performance of which the law in some way recognizes as a duty." Simply put, a contract is a promise accepted by the person to whom it is made. If Friendly Frank agrees to sell you a 1967 Chevy from his used-car lot for $400, and you accept, a contract is formed.

The two crucial elements of a contract are agreement and obligation. Each party to a contract has an obligation to give up something, usually goods or services on the part of the seller and money on the part of the buyer. An agreement is said to exist when the buyer and seller have a meeting of minds on exactly what each party to the contract is obliged to give up.

However, there is sometimes a disparity between a person's

real intention and the intention he or she makes known to the other party. Today the courts seem to prefer an objective theory of contract law, which says that the real intention is the intention made known to the other party. Suppose your neighbor says, "I'll sell you this lawnmower for $60," intending to say $70. If you accept the offer, a contract is formed for $60—despite the fact that the neighbor intended to sell the lawnmower for $10 more.

Offers which appear in newspaper advertisements are usually considered to be invitations to enter into negotiations rather than as firm offers, particularly when the newspaper makes a mistake in the advertisement. Suppose a department store submits an ad which reads, "Color Television Sets, $400," and the newspaper omits the final zero and runs an ad which states, "Color Television Sets, $40." The store is not required to sell the television sets at the printed price.

Not every promise or set of promises creates a legal obligation. An agreement which is based *only* on goodwill or natural affection will not be enforced. If, for example, Frank and Angela agree to meet in front of the Waverly Theater at a certain time, no legal obligation is created, since it is clear that the two friends intend a social obligation and not a contract.

Must a Contract Be in Writing?

Most people assume that a contract must be in writing. As a consequence, when a person is deprived of his rights, he is frequently heard to complain, "If I only had it in writing." Actually, oral contracts are valid and enforceable in many circumstances.

In most states an oral contract for the sale of goods is valid and enforceable if the sale is for less than $500. For example, if you make an oral agreement to purchase a color television set for $400, the agreement is enforceable. If you agree orally to purchase the television set for $600, the agreement is not enforceable. However, if goods are being specially manufactured for you and are not suitable for sale to others in the ordinary course of business, the contract will be valid even if it is not in writing. This rarely applies to consumer goods, since most automobiles, television sets, etc. are suitable for sale to others. Also, when the seller has received and accepted payment for the goods, a valid contract exists, although not in writing. Suppose that your neighbor agrees to sell you his automobile for $2,000, and you pay him the agreed-upon amount. Later that day he tells you that he wants to cancel the deal because he has another buyer who is willing to pay $2,500. There is a valid contract between you and your neighbor which can be enforced even though it is not in writing.

If the contract involves services rather than goods, the contract must be in writing to be enforceable. However, there are exceptions to this rule. A contract that can be performed within one year is valid even if it is not in writing, and it is obvious that most oral agreements are simple agreements which are capable of being performed within a year. In most states an oral agreement is also valid if there is a partial performance by one party. This is considered evidence that the parties intended to make an agreement. If you agree to paint your neighbor's fence for $50 and complete half the work, there is a valid and enforceable agreement.

Finally, a contract must be in writing if it involves the sale of real property or the lease of real property for a certain period of time, ordinarily one year.

Must a Contract Follow a Fixed Form?

The law does not require that a written contract be in any particular form. It can be in the form of a printed sales agreement, a memorandum, or a letter. In fact, a contract can be written on a tablecloth in a restaurant. (There are limits, however. No one has yet suggested that you close a deal by writing the contract in the sand at the beach.) When attempting to enforce a contract, however, bear in mind that a contract can be enforced only against a party who has signed it. If you want another person to be bound by the terms of a written agreement, then you had better be certain that he signs it.

Negotiating the Terms of a Contract

Since consumer contracts are drawn up by the merchant (or his attorney), with no opportunity for the consumer to negotiate more favorable terms, they are very much "take it or leave it" propositions. As one law professor wrote:

". . . much of 19th-Century contract law was predicated upon the model of a contract between two parties of relatively equal bargaining power who negotiate and conclude a mutually accept-able agreement. Instead, the bulk of contracts today are various forms of adhesion contracts, the mass-produced, nonnegotiated contracts pioneered by the insurance, utilities and transportation industries. The consent in these adhesion contracts is a fiction. The party handed a form usually has no time to read it, would not understand it if he took the time, and would not be able to find anyone with authority to change it if he wished to, and very likely would not be able to make the transaction if he insisted upon a change from the standard form" (Justin Sweet, *Liqui-dated Damages in California*, 60 CALIFORNIA LAW REVIEW 85).

As a result, many consumers simply throw up their hands and sign whatever document is placed before them. It is a distressing fact that consumers often sign contracts without even glancing at the terms and conditions. The reason that most consumers give for this practice is that they cannot understand the legal jargon anyway, so why waste time trying.

Many contracts do contain provisions couched in abstruse legal jargon. However, there is a trend to simplify the content of consumer agreements. A number of companies have voluntarily changed the terms of their contracts and loan agreements to remove unnecessary legal language. New York State has passed a new law which requires contracts for consumer goods and ser-vices to be written in nontechnical language and in "a clear and coherent manner using words with common and everyday mean-ings."

In any case, however, it is always advisable to read a contract thoroughly before signing it. Some contracts have a printed clause above the signature line: "Buyer has read the agreement and agrees to all terms and conditions printed on the reverse side hereof." So be sure to turn the agreement over and read what is on the reverse side, or you may be agreeing to something that was never discussed orally. If you find some provision in the contract that makes the transaction unacceptable, you can insist that the provision be changed before you go ahead with the deal. If the contract is changed, make certain that both you and the other party initial the change.

On the other hand, there may have been an oral agreement which is left out of the contract. The seller is protected by a clause in the contract which reads, "There are no agreements or conditions between the parties other than those specifically set forth in this contract." But what protects you? Suppose the seller agrees orally to provide free service for a year or to deliver the product to your home. In most cases, these promises are not binding unless they are made part of the written agreement. So read the contract and its terms carefully to be sure that all the seller's promises are specifically included. If not, insist that they be added before you sign.

Reading the Small Print

Most consumer contracts are printed on a form with the seller's name at the top, followed by blank spaces for the name, address, and telephone number of the buyer. There is usually also a space for the salesperson's name. Be sure it is filled in legibly. If a question of fraud or misrepresentation ever develops, you will want to know the name of the person who gave you information about the product.

The middle section of a contract is usually set aside for a description of the goods. Insist that the description include the brand name and model number. If it is a bedroom set, it should include the color, as well as an itemized list of the pieces. This is to make clear that the agreement pertains to the specific merchandise that you purchased, and to make certain that you receive everything you paid for.

If the seller cannot give you the merchandise at the time of the sale, be sure that a delivery date is specified on the contract— before you make a down payment. Sometimes delivery may take longer than anticipated. In the furniture industry it is not uncommon for a manufacturer to deliver pieces six months or even a year after an order is placed. In New York City a furniture store is required by law to write an estimated delivery date conspicuously on the contract, and if the store cannot deliver within 30 days of the date, the customer has the option to cancel the contract and obtain a complete refund. But even if you live outside of New York, make certain that the merchant specifies a delivery date—in writing.

A contract for the sale of goods may include a number of *express warranties* or guarantees. These warranties are created in several ways:

1. If the seller makes a statement about the goods and that statement becomes part of the basis of the agreement, the seller is specifically guaranteeing that that statement is true.
2. If the seller describes the goods and the buyer makes the purchase on the basis of that description, the seller is expressly warranting that the goods will conform to the description.
3. If the buyer makes a purchase on the basis of a sample or model, the seller is guaranteeing that the goods will conform to the sample or model.

These warranties may be created by written as well as oral statements. There may be an express warranty even though the seller does not use the specific words "warranty" or "guarantee."

Concerning warranties, there is some good news and some bad news. The good news is that every contract for the sale of goods carries certain *implied warranties*. These warranties exist even though they are not expressly declared. There is an implied *warranty of title*—that is, that the seller has clear ownership of the goods. Under this warranty, you are assured that the seller has a right to sell the goods and that the goods are free from any liens or encumbrances. There is also an implied *warranty of merchantability* if the seller is a merchant who sells goods of that kind. Under this warranty the seller promises that the goods will be fit for the ordinary purpose for which such goods are used, that the goods will be adequately packaged and labeled, and that the goods will conform to the promises on the package. When you purchase a stereo set from a local dealer, the dealer warrants that the set will be fit for the ordinary purpose for which such goods are used, which in this case means playing stereophonic records. There can also be an implied *warranty of fitness* for a particular purpose. When the seller at the time the contract is made has reason to know of the particular use for which the goods are required and the buyer relies on the seller's skill or judgment to select suitable goods, there is an implied warranty that the goods shall be fit for such purpose. These warranties can be cited by consumers who receive defective merchandise.

Now for the bad news. The seller may exclude or modify the implied warranties. To exclude or modify the implied warranty of merchantability the language must mention merchantability and in the case of a written agreement must be conspicuous. To exclude or modify any implied warranty of fitness, the exclusion must be in writing and conspicuous. Language to exclude all implied warranties of fitness is sufficient if it states, for example, "There are no warranties which extend beyond the description on the face hereof." Unless the circumstances indicate otherwise, all implied warranties are excluded by expressions like "as is," "with all faults," or other language which in common understanding calls the buyer's attention to the exclusion of warranties and makes plain that there is no implied warranty. In addition, when the buyer has examined the goods or the sample as fully as he desires, or has refused to examine the goods, there is no implied warranty with regard to defects which an examination ought to have revealed to him.

A contract may also contain provisions regarding refunds or returns. These are particularly important with regard to items of clothing. In New York City, when a store does not permit refunds, it must post this policy on a sign located at the point of display, the cash register, or the store entrance.

The contract or sales agreement may also contain provisions about payment. When payment is not made in advance, the contract may call for a minimum deposit. Some contracts may also make the claim, in small print, that the contract is noncancellable or that the buyer forfeits the deposit in the event of cancellation. These provisions may be illegal (as shown later in this chapter) but it is still a good idea to make the smallest possible down payment. Once the seller has all or a substantial portion of the contract price, it may be difficult to convince the seller to return the money without filing a lawsuit.

At the bottom of the contract there is usually a space for the buyer's signature. If the contract price is to be paid in installments, the seller may ask for a *cosigner*. A cosigner is usually a friend or relative who assumes the responsibility for making the payments if the buyer fails to do so. This arrangement seems to benefit everybody but the cosigner. The buyer has the product. The seller has an additional party—usually with a good credit rating—to assure payment. But the cosigner is left with the legal obligation to pay the balance due if, for some reason, the buyer defaults. And when that happens the cosigner usually hears about it for the first time when a process server suddenly shows up with a summons.

One final note about contractual terms: If you don't understand a contract, and if the contract involves a substantial sum of money, consult an attorney.

Consumer Defenses

Fortunately, most contracts work out well, with both parties usually getting pretty much what they expected out of the transaction. Sometimes, however, the buyer is deceived by the seller or pays an exorbitant price for shoddy and defective merchandise. In recent years the courts have shown a greater interest in protecting the rights of consumers in such situations. As one court noted: "No longer do we believe that fraud may be perpetrated by the cry of *caveat emptor*. We have reached the point where 'let the buyer beware' is a poor business philosophy for a social order allegedly based upon man's respect for his fellow man. Let the seller beware, too! A free enterprise system not founded upon personal morality will ultimately lose freedom."

If there is a dispute between the parties, great weight will be given to the terms of the written contract. However, it is widely recognized, as noted earlier, that most consumer contracts are drafted by the seller, for the benefit of the seller, at the expense of the buyer. The general view is that the contract should be strictly enforced against the party who drafted it. If the language is vague or ambiguous, the court may interpret it in a fashion which will protect the weaker party.

The most common defenses used by consumers to protect themselves from the consequences of an unfair contract are outlined below.

Fraud. One basic consumer defense is a claim of fraud. To prove fraud the buyer must show: (1) that the seller made a statement of fact, (2) that the statement was false and known by the seller to be false at the time it was made, (3) that the seller made the false statement with intent to deceive the buyer, (4) that the buyer relied upon the seller's statement, and (5) that the buyer sustained damages as a result of that reliance.

An obvious example of fraud would be when a dealer tells a buyer that a used television set is new. The buyer, accepting the statement as true, purchases the set. When the buyer returns home he finds that the set does not work well and calls a repairman. The repairman tells him that the major parts in the set are at least five years old. In such a case the buyer can sue the seller for fraud and recover the amount paid for the set.

What happens when a seller's statement or promise is not made part of the written agreement? In general, the courts will not permit oral testimony to contradict the terms of a written contract. This is called the *parol evidence* rule. However, the courts will usually take oral evidence if one party claims a fraudulent statement was made.

Generally sales talk, or what is commonly referred to as "puffing," is not considered to be fraud. When a salesman says, "This is the best TV on the market," the buyer should consider this as an expression of the seller's opinion only, and not the basis for a charge of fraud.

Rescission. A buyer may annul or rescind a contract if the seller made a misstatement of some material fact. This differs from fraud in that the buyer need only show that the misstatement was made, not that it was made intentionally. An example will clarify the difference:

When Susan Jones enrolled in a vocational training school, she told the registrar that she had to take her courses in the evening so that the classes would not interfere with her job. When she was told that the courses would be offered at 8:00 P.M., she signed the agreement and left a deposit of $200. Several days later she was notified that she had been assigned to classes beginning at 10:00 each morning. When she called the registrar's office, she was told that the school was unable to schedule evening classes. When she complained, the school told her that they would not return the $200 deposit. Since Susan Jones was induced to sign the agreement on the basis of the representation about evening classes, she has a basis for rescinding the agreement and recovering her deposit.

A contract can also be rescinded if it contains provisions which are illegal or contrary to public policy. This may be the case with contracts which purport to be "noncancellable," or which severely restrict the consumer's right to cancel. As a general rule, the consumer can cancel the contract before the seller has provided goods or services, if he is willing to pay the seller's damages. And the seller's damages, at this stage, usually amount to a small portion of the contract price.

The Uniform Commercial Code, which applies to the sale of goods such as automobiles and television sets, states that an agreement can provide for damages if one of the parties breaches the contract. However, the amount of the damages must be reasonable—considering the anticipated or actual harm, the difficulty of proving loss, and the inconvenience or impossibility of obtaining an adequate remedy. When the amount specified is unreasonably large, far exceeding the actual damages incurred, it will usually be considered a penalty and therefore void.

What is a reasonable amount? A contractual provision that fixes damages at 20% will probably be considered fair, while a clause that sets damages at 50% will most likely be considered a penalty.

Although contracts for services—such as dance lessons or vocational training courses—are not governed by the Uniform Commercial Code, the same general rules apply. If the cancellation fee in the contract is too high, the court may consider it a penalty and refuse to enforce the contract.

In one case, a woman signed a contract with a health spa to pay $300 for 190 weight-reducing sessions. The contract provided that "the sessions purchased are not transferable, refundable, or cancellable." When the woman tried to cancel the contract, the health spa sued for $300, the full amount due under the contract. The court ruled that the contract clause prohibiting cancellation was a penalty clause: "This type of contract clause which demands full payment of the contract price even when no services are performed and no loss proven is unconscionable and will not be enforced by the court."

Recently, a number of states have passed laws governing the amount of money that can be charged when a consumer contract is canceled. New York State, for example, now has such laws regarding dance lessons and vocational training courses. Obviously, any contract that does not comply with state law may be declared illegal.

Unconscionability. The courts have refused to enforce unconscionable contracts—that is, contracts so harsh and unreasonable as to be shocking to the conscience. They have done so in a limited number of cases where (1) there was gross inequality of bargaining power, (2) the consumer was unsophisticated and unable to speak English fluently, and (3) there was a wide disparity between the contract price and the actual value of the goods or services purchased. In one case, for example, the court held that a contract to purchase a food freezer for $1,439 was unconscionable because the buyer was a welfare recipient unfamiliar with commercial transactions and the contract price was three times the actual value of the freezer.

Breach of Contract. When one party does not perform according to the terms of an agreement, the other party can sue for breach of contract.

In one breach of contract case, a young woman sued a career school because the school was unable to place her in a job after she completed the course of study. The school's advertising material indicated that it had placed 97% of its graduates with major airlines, and that "if you are accepted you may rest easy about your future in the fascinating airlines field." The judge ruled that such statements were an inducement to the young woman to enroll in the school and constituted an implied guarantee of employment, and that the school's failure to perform as promised amounted to a breach of contract.

A person who purchases goods may also sue for breach of contract. If the goods are delivered in defective or damaged condition, the suit is really one for breach of warranty. In these cases, the buyer may sue to recover the difference between the value of the goods delivered and the value they would have had if they had been delivered as promised.

A buyer may also reject the goods and rescind the contract. Under the provisions of the Uniform Commercial Code, a buyer must be given a reasonable opportunity to inspect the goods before acceptance and, if the goods fail in any way to conform to the contract, to reject them. If the goods are obviously defective at the time of delivery, the buyer should refuse to accept the goods. But if the defect is not apparent until afterward—and this may happen with carpeting or furniture—it is the obligation of the buyer to notify the seller within a reasonable time that the goods do not meet the terms of the contract. If you do this with a phone call, you should also follow up with a letter and keep a copy of the letter in your files. It is not your responsibility to return the defective merchandise, but only to hold it with reasonable care and to make it available for a time sufficient for the seller to remove it.

Under certain circumstances, the seller is given the opportunity to "cure" the defects: (1) when the contract specifies a time for performance, and the seller is able to substitute conforming merchandise within that time; or (2) when the seller had reasonable grounds to believe the nonconforming merchandise would be acceptable and is able to substitute a conforming order within a reasonable time.

If the buyer accepts defective merchandise because the seller promised to cure the defect, but the seller has not done so within a reasonable time, the buyer can revoke that acceptance, if it can be shown that there was *a substantial impairment of value*.

Consumers who have been stuck with a "lemon" may find some comfort in this story:

A buyer bought a new automobile from a dealer in Alabama. During the first year the buyer had the car, it was brought in for repairs about thirty times. Despite extensive work the car continued to operate poorly. The frustrated buyer then brought suit against the dealer. The court ruled that he had a right to rescind the contract and that any acceptance made could be revoked since there was "a substantial impairment of value."

Remember that a dealer can try to disclaim or limit any warranties. But to be effective the disclaimer or limitation must be conspicuous. In the automobile case mentioned above, the court refused to honor the seller's disclaimer of warranty because it appeared in the owner's manual and the owner's manual was not given to the buyer until after the sale.

Consumer Protection Regulations

Consumers may benefit from a number of federal or state laws that prohibit deceptive or unfair trade practices. There is not sufficient space in this book to list all of such laws and regulations, but you should be aware of some of the most important ones.

Because many consumers, particularly low-income consumers, were victimized by high-pressure door-to-door salesmen, the Federal Trade Commission passed a regulation giving consumers a three-day "cooling-off period" to cancel their purchases. The regulation requires that any door-to-door sales contract or receipt must have attached to it a Notice of Cancellation (see sample, p. 17). The regulation covers the sale, lease, or rental of consumer goods or services with a purchase price of $25 or more (thus exempting the sale of Girl Scout cookies). The regulation does not apply to sales conducted and consummated entirely by telephone.

Consumers who purchase used automobiles usually rely on the odometer reading as an index of the condition and value of the automobile. Congress has recently passed a law prohibiting anyone from disconnecting, resetting, or altering the odometer so as to change the number of miles. The seller must also give a written statement to the buyer disclosing the cumulative mileage registered on the car and indicating that the actual mileage is unknown if the seller knows the odometer reading to differ from the number of miles actually traveled. Any person who violates this law with intent to defraud may be sued by the buyer for three times the amount of actual damages or $1,500, whichever is greater. And when the buyer is successful, he may recover the court costs, together with reasonable attorney fees.

Some businesses—such as home-improvement contractors, vocational schools, and automobile repair shops—are licensed by state or city agencies, and the agency granting the license may adopt regulations governing the form and content of consumer contracts. New York City's Department of Consumer Affairs, for example, has adopted regulations that provide consumers with three days in which to cancel home-improvement contracts.

NOTICE OF CANCELLATION

---

date [enter date of transaction]

YOU MAY CANCEL THIS TRANSACTION WITHOUT ANY PENALTY OR OBLIGATION, WITHIN THREE BUSINESS DAYS FROM THE ABOVE DATE.

IF YOU CANCEL, ANY PROPERTY TRADED IN, ANY PAYMENTS MADE BY YOU UNDER THE CONTRACT OR SALE, AND ANY NEGOTIABLE INSTRUMENT EXECUTED BY YOU WILL BE RETURNED WITHIN TEN BUSINESS DAYS FOLLOWING RECEIPT BY THE SELLER OF YOUR CANCELLATION NOTICE, AND ANY SECURITY INTEREST ARISING OUT OF THE TRANSACTION WILL BE CANCELLED.

※　※　※

TO CANCEL THIS TRANSACTION, MAIL OR DELIVER A SIGNED AND DATED COPY OF THIS CANCELLATION NOTICE OR ANY OTHER WRITTEN NOTICE, OR SEND A TELEGRAM, TO [name of seller], AT [address of seller's place of business] NOT LATER THAN MIDNIGHT OF

---

date

I HEREBY CANCEL THIS TRANSACTION.

---

date   Buyer's signature

If you have a dispute with a company, it is a good idea to see if the company is licensed by a governmental agency. If so, the agency may help you resolve the dispute or provide you with information about your legal rights.

Credit Purchases

Many people decide to purchase consumer goods on credit. A credit purchase is one in which the customer buys now and defers payment until later. When you purchase goods at a department store with a credit card or when you purchase an automobile and make payments in installments, you are buying on credit. The amount of credit now granted by businesses and financial institutions is staggering. For every man, woman, and child in this country there is approximately $1,500 outstanding in consumer credit.

The terms of a credit transaction are not always clear to a consumer. What does it mean to say, "You can pay us on credit," or "Interest at 8%"? At one time, consumers who wanted to purchase on credit were easily confused by the different methods used to compute interest rates. Since there was no standard method used to let consumers know the real cost of the credit sale, it was impossible to compare interest.

Today, however, credit transactions are governed by the Consumer Credit Protection Act, commonly referred to as "Truth-in-Lending." The act was passed by Congress to make it possible for consumers to understand and compare credit terms, to avoid the uninformed use of credit, and to guard against inaccurate and unfair credit billing and credit-card practices. It requires that all sellers disclose the cost of consumer credit and that those credit terms be made a part of the contract between the buyer and the seller.

Credit Cards. Credit cards issued by department stores, banks, credit-card companies, and even oil companies are sometimes referred to as revolving charge accounts. This means that each new purchase made with the card is simply added to the outstanding balance. When the bill is received, it can be paid either in full or in monthly installments. If it is paid in full, there will probably be no finance charges, although some banks charge a service fee, and American Express charges an annual membership fee. But if the bill is paid in monthly installments, there will usually also be a finance charge. The finance charge is the sum of all charges imposed by the seller for the extension of credit, including service and carrying charges, loan fees, investigation or credit-report fees, and charges for life or accident insurance to cover the outstanding credit.

The finance charges levied by the credit-card company, expressed as an annual percentage rate, usually appear on both the application form and the monthly statement. The annual percentage rate is the relative cost of credit expressed in percentage terms. The annual percentage rate is usually 18% a year or 1½% a month.

With over 500 million credit cards now in use, it is not difficult to imagine how individual purchases can get lost in the shuffle. A consumer reading a bill may not be able to remember what items were purchased at the shopping mall six weeks earlier. Under the provisions of Truth-in-Lending, the credit-card company is required to include with each bill a brief description of the goods or services purchased.

Retail Installment Contract. Consumers sometimes make credit purchases without using a credit card or a revolving charge account. A consumer who purchases an automobile on credit, for example, will probably sign a retail contract providing for payments to be made in equal monthly installments. Under the provisions of Truth-in-Lending, the dealer must disclose the cost of the credit before the transaction is completed and the contract signed.

Look at the sample retail installment contract for the purchase of a new car, on the following page. The contract provides specific information about the following items:

1. *Cash price*. This is the price at which the creditor offers, in the ordinary course of doing business, to sell the goods or services. In this case, the cash price is the sticker price of the car plus the cost of any extras ordered by the buyer.

2. *Cash down payment*. The creditor is required to list the cash price, less any cash down payment. The customer has made a $500 cash down payment.

3. *Trade-in*. This is the value of the property transferred to the creditor. In this case, the customer has agreed to trade in his 1975 car for $1,400.

RETAIL INSTALLMENT CONTRACT AND SECURITY AGREEMENT

Seller's Name: **Friendly Frank**
Brooklyn, N.Y.

Contract # **1001**

The undersigned (herein called Buyer, whether one or more) purchases from **F. Frank** (seller) and grants to **Seller** a security interest in, subject to the terms and conditions hereof, the following described property.

BUYER'S NAME **John Smith**
BUYER'S ADDRESS **52 Baker St.**
CITY **Brooklyn** STATE **N.Y.** ZIP____

1. CASH PRICE		$ **6,200**
2. LESS: CASH DOWN PAYMENT	$ **500**	
3. TRADE-IN	**1,400**	
4. TOTAL DOWN PAYMENT	**1,900**	$ **1,900**
5. UNPAID BALANCE OF CASH PRICE		$ **4,300**
6. OTHER CHARGES: **title certificate**		$ **5**
7. AMOUNT FINANCED		$ **4,305**
8. FINANCE CHARGE		$ **609**
9. TOTAL OF PAYMENTS		$ **4,914**
10. DEFERRED PAYMENT PRICE (1+6+8)		$ **6,814**
11. ANNUAL PERCENTAGE RATE		**13.10** %

QUANTITY	DESCRIPTION	AMOUNT	
1	**New automobile**	**6200**	**00**
	with radio and		
	white wall tires.		
Description of Trade-in:			
1975 automobile		**1400**	**00**

Insurance Agreement

The purchase of insurance coverage is voluntary and not required for credit. _____ Insurance coverage is available at a cost of $ _____ for the term of credit.

I desire insurance coverage

Signed_____ Date_____

I do not desire insurance coverage

Signed_____ Date_____

Buyer hereby agrees to pay to **Seller** _____ at their offices shown above the "TOTAL OF PAYMENTS" shown above in **24** monthly installments of $**204.75** (final payment to be $**204.75** the first installment being payable **June 1** 19**80** and all subsequent installments on the same day of each consecutive month until paid in full.)

NOTICE TO BUYER: 1. Do not sign this contract before you read it or if it contains any blank space. 2. You are entitled to a completely filled in copy of this contract when you sign it. 3. Under the law, you have the following rights, among others: (a) To pay off in advance the full amount due and to obtain a partial refund of the credit service charge; (b) To redeem the property if repossessed for default; (c) To require, under certain conditions, a resale of the property if repossessed. 4. According to law you have the privilege of purchasing the insurance on the motor vehicle provided for in this contract from an agent or broker of your own selection. (See additional terms on reverse side.)

THIS IS A RETAIL INSTALLMENT CONTRACT.
RECEIPT OF AN EXECUTED COPY IS ACKNOWLEDGED.

SELLER'S NAME **Friendly Frank** BUYER_____

Accepted by _____

4. *Total down payment*. This is the total of the cash down payment and the trade-in.

5. *Unpaid balance of cash price*. This is the difference between the cash price (Item 1) and the total down payment (Item 4).

6. *Other charges*. The creditor is required to list all other charges that are not part of the finance charge. In this case, the dealer has added a $5 fee for filing the Certificate of Title.

7. *Amount financed*. This is the balance owed by the customer before the interest charges are added.

8. *Finance charges*. The creditor must disclose (in dollars) the amount of interest and carrying charges.

9. *Total of payments*. This is the sum of all payments due.

10. *Deferred payment price*. This is the sum of Items 1, 6, and 8 above.

11. *Annual percentage rate*. This is the cost of credit expressed in percentage terms. The maximum rate is set by state law.

The words "finance charge" and "annual percentage rate" are printed in bold letters so as to be more conspicuous than other terms in the contract.

There may be a special provision in the contract giving the seller a *security interest* in the goods, which means that the seller may repossess the goods if the buyer defaults or stops making payments.

Consumers who buy on credit must always be alert for hidden finance charges. In one case a health spa had almost all of its customers sign promissory notes or retail installment contracts, showing "none" for the finance charge and "0%" for the annual percentage rate. As it turned out, however, the health spa sold the notes and contracts to a bank at a 16% discount—that is, the bank paid the spa the face amount of the notes, less 16%. The court found that the spa was concealing the real cost of credit. The "cash price" of the contract was really the amount received by the spa from the bank, and the 16% discount represented a finance charge that should have been disclosed to the customer under Truth-in-Lending.

A creditor who fails to comply with any requirement of the Truth-in-Lending Act is liable for an amount equal to twice the amount of the finance charge, except that the liability cannot be less than $100 or more than $1,000. The court may also award court costs and reasonable attorney's fees. A creditor is not liable, however, if it can be proved that the violation was not intentional and that the creditor had set up reasonable procedures to avoid such an error. But the creditor will probably have a difficult time proving this to the satisfaction of the court.

There is a one-year statute of limitations for Truth-in-Lending claims, which means that a customer must bring an action within one year of the violation. When a creditor sues a customer for failure to make payments, however, the customer can make a counterclaim based on any Truth-in-Lending violation in the contract, in which case there is no statute of limitations.

While it is true that most retail stores and banks have expert legal counsel to advise them on Truth-in-Lending, the provisions of the law are extremely technical and violations do occur. So look closely at the finance charge and make certain that you understand the real cost of credit before signing on the dotted line.

3

Leasing an Apartment

Most people who sign a lease for an apartment do so without thoroughly reviewing it. This may be because they find the language of the lease, as with most contracts, to be incomprehensible. Or it may be that they do not want to risk antagonizing the landlord by questioning certain terms of the lease for fear he will rent the apartment to some more agreeable tenant.

This is a mistake, because signing a lease represents a considerable financial commitment. If, for example, you agree to rent an apartment for two years for $500 a month, you are making a commitment to pay $12,000 during the term of the lease. With so much money at stake, you should have a clear understanding of your legal rights and obligations when you enter into such an agreement.

A lease is an agreement between the landlord and the tenant which conveys to the tenant not the ownership of the property, but the right to occupy it for a certain period of time.

In general, there are two types of leases. An agreement to rent an apartment or some other place to live is usually called a *residential lease*. An agreement to rent a store or office, on the other hand, is usually called a *commercial lease*. If you sign a residential lease, it will probably specify that the property may be used only as a "strictly private dwelling." The landlord would then have the right to object if you used the apartment as a store or fashion boutique. But can the landlord protest if you occasionally use the apartment to entertain friends or if you allow a guest to stay overnight?

In one New York case, a landlord tried to evict a female tenant because she had used the apartment for "illicit relations." The tenant was not a prostitute, but had engaged in sexual intercourse, from time to time, with one particular man.

"The question for decision," stated the judge, "is whether chastity is a prerequisite to maintenance of the landlord-tenant relationship." The judge ruled that the tenant had done nothing illegal since the law of New York did not prohibit normal sexual intercourse carried out in private between unmarried consenting adults.

"So much for illegality," remarked the judge. "With respect to immorality, one should say little. . . . If the test be personal to me, I hold that, without a showing—and there is none—that she has harmed anyone, [the tenant] has done nothing immoral. And if the test be the response of the 'ordinary' or 'average' man or woman, assuming that it makes sense to posit the existence of such a person, I hold that, given the ethical standards of the day, [the tenant] has done nothing immoral."

The judge concluded that acts of sexual intercourse between unmarried consenting adults, which do not involve public disorder or prostitution, do not constitute a basis for eviction.

Some landlords try to screen their tenants before they move in. They may ask for certain financial information or for an application form to be filled out. But most cities and states have antidiscrimination laws which prohibit a landlord from screening applicants on the basis of race, religion, or sex. It may also be illegal in some places to deny a tenant an apartment because he is handicapped.

Reading the Lease

A lease consists of a series of promises made between the landlord and the tenant. It is possible to have an oral lease—at least for a short period of time—but in many states an oral lease for more than one year is invalid.

Your landlord will usually insist on a written lease, and will use a standard form prepared by a realty association or landlord group. The lease may consist of several thousand words—in small print—but it is important that you read it thoroughly before signing. There may be provisions barring pets or requiring you to pay for certain repairs or other expenses which you cannot accept no matter how much you like the apartment.

When you read the lease, you should pay careful attention to the following provisions:

The term of the lease. The lease should specify the period of time it is going to run, indicating the exact dates on which the lease begins and ends. Check the dates carefully. Otherwise you may find that you have signed a one-year lease when you bargained for two years.

Monthly rental. The lease should disclose the total amount of money to be paid during the term of the lease and the amount of each monthly payment. Check the numbers to be certain they are correct. The monthly rental times the number of months should equal the total amount to be paid under the lease. Make sure the figure you agreed to orally is the figure that appears in the lease. If you sign a lease to pay $440 a month, you will have difficulty proving that you had an oral agreement to pay $400.

Security deposit. Most landlords insist on obtaining a security deposit from the tenant when the lease is signed. The amount of the deposit should be stated in the lease. If the tenant moves out and leaves the apartment in shambles, the landlord can use all or part of the security deposit to pay for the restoration of the apartment. In New York, the landlord must place the security deposit in a bank account and inform the tenant of the name of the bank. If there are at least six apartments in the building, the landlord must add interest on the amount held on deposit (less 1% for administrative expenses).

Service and repairs. The lease should specify any services the landlord has agreed to supply. If the landlord has agreed to pay for gas, electricity, or other utilities, that fact should be clearly stated in the lease. If the landlord has agreed to provide a dishwasher or air conditioner, make certain that too is in the lease. The lease should also state who is responsible for repairing fixtures and electrical wiring, and whether or not you need the landlord's permission before installing paneling or making other improvements.

Rules and regulations. The lease may have a special section with rules governing the conduct of the tenants. For example, the landlord may have established rules regarding the use of the laundry room, or when you may or may not play your stereo or radio. Another rule may prohibit your installing new locks or burglar alarms without the landlord's permission. You may not be able to get any of the rules changed, but it's certainly a good idea to know what the rules are before you move in.

Additional promises. Before you sign the lease, the landlord may tell you that he intends to paint the apartment, or, if parking

[25]

is a problem in the neighborhood, he may offer you space in the garage. The landlord should agree to put such promises in the lease. (It is not advisable to rely on an oral promise by the landlord or the building superintendent even if you think the promise has been made in good faith.) Many leases contain a provision to the effect that "there are no promises, representations or warranties other than those specifically set forth in the lease." If you have relied on an oral promise and the landlord refuses to honor it, you may have to take your complaint to court. And you may not be able to win in court unless you can prove fraud—which is never an easy thing to do.

Unfortunately, many leases are written in technical language that only a legal scholar could decipher. A typical lease may state: "Lessee or the legal representative of the Lessee shall pay Lessor as the liquidated damages for the failure of Lessee to observe and perform said Lessee's convenants herein contained, any deficiency between the rent hereby reserved and/or covenanted to be paid and the net amount, if any, of the rents collected on account of the lease or leases of the demised premises for each month of the period which would otherwise have constituted the balance of the term of the lease."

Obviously, it is unfair to expect tenants to protect their legal rights if they cannot even understand the documents they are signing. For this reason, New York State has passed a law requiring leases to be written in plain English. This means that the lease must be written in nontechnical language and in a clear and coherent manner, using words with common and everyday meanings. (New legal forms have been prepared changing words like "lessor" and "lessee" to "landlord" and "tenant"; the phrase "demised premises" has been simplified to "the apartment.") A landlord who violates this law can be penalized $50 and required to pay for any loss that a tenant suffers as a result of the violation. However, this does not mean that the lease is automatically void. It is still valid and enforceable even if the landlord has to pay damages to the tenant.

As a practical matter, most tenants have very little bargaining power. Since residential leases are usually prepared by a lawyer representing the landlord or by a real estate association, it is a good bet that most of the provisions are designed to protect the landlord's interests. In major cities, where housing is scarce, the landlord clearly has the upper hand. If a prospective tenant refuses to sign an unfair or one-sided lease, the landlord knows that there are other people waiting in line to take the apartment and that most of them will be willing to accept the lease without argument. The fact that the landlord can dictate the terms is now widely recognized, and many states have passed new laws prohibiting the use of certain lease provisions which are unjust or unfair.

Many leases contain a clause which states that the landlord is not liable if a tenant is injured on the premises, even if the injury is a result of the landlord's negligence. In many states, such as New York, these provisions are contrary to state law and are therefore void.

Some leases contain a provision for "liquidated damages," which is a specified amount—one or two months' rent, for example—due the landlord in the event the tenant violates the terms of the agreement. Courts sometimes refuse to enforce these provisions if the amount is too high or if it does not bear any reasonable relation to the actual amount of damages anticipated by the landlord.

Sometimes there is a clause which states that whenever the landlord files suit to enforce the lease, the tenant must pay the landlord's attorney's fees. This type of clause is often enforced by the courts. In New York, however, if the lease gives the landlord the right to obtain attorney's fees, the tenant automatically gets the same right. If the tenant sues the landlord and wins, or successfully defends a suit brought by the landlord, then the landlord must pay the tenant's attorney's fees.

New York State also has a new law which provides that a court may refuse to enforce a lease which is *unconscionable* (or so unfair or unjust that it offends the conscience). Under this law, a judge who finds that a lease is unconscionable can do one of the following: (1) he can refuse to enforce the lease, (2) he can enforce the remainder of the lease without the unconscionable clause, or (3) he can limit the application of the unconscionable clause so as to avoid any unconscionable result. In one case, decided even before the law was passed, several tenants sued a landlord to collect damages because the landlord had not provided air conditioning as promised in the lease. The landlord claimed that he could not be sued and cited a provision in the lease stating that "interruption or curtailment of any service shall not . . . subject landlord to any liability for damages or otherwise." After reading the lease, the judge remarked, "If we cannot construe this agreement in accordance with the honorable intentions of fair-minded people, we are left with a one-sided disclaimer of liability which denies the tenants redress in the courts for the landlord's breach of a binding promise to supply essential services, including air conditioning." The judge ruled that the provision in the lease shielding the landlord from liability was unconscionable and unenforceable.

Your Rights as a Tenant

Once you have signed a lease and moved into an apartment, what are your rights and privileges?

First of all, you have the right to occupy and enjoy the apartment without being disturbed by the landlord or the other tenants. This right is implied in every lease and is usually referred to as the *right of quiet enjoyment*. This means that if the landlord decides that he doesn't like you and wants you out of the building, he cannot create a disturbance outside your apartment every day to try to force you to leave.

More complicated problems arise when the noise or interference is caused by another tenant. If a tenant is causing a disturbance, the best tactic is to approach the tenant directly, in a peaceful and calm manner, to try to persuade him to do something to reduce the noise. If this does not work, you can then complain to the landlord. As a general rule, landlords do not like to get involved in squabbles between tenants. However, if enough people complain, the landlord may speak to the offending tenant and, if the annoyance does not stop, may even try to evict the tenant.

Most people would agree, however, that eviction is a drastic step to take against a tenant who has a few loud parties or who occasionally makes too much noise. People who live in a city apartment cannot expect to eliminate all signs of life. As one judge remarked, "The peace and quiet of a rural estate or the sylvan silence of a mountain lodge cannot be expected in a multiple dwelling."

As a general rule, a tenant's conduct becomes objectionable if it is unreasonable or unlawful to the annoyance, inconvenience, discomfort, or damage of others. If a dispute between a landlord and a tenant goes to court, the judge must balance the competing interests of the parties, as the following case demonstrates:

Mr. and Mrs. Carlton lived in an apartment in Manhattan. Their fifteen-year-old son liked to play the drums. When some of the neighbors complained about the noise, the landlord wrote a letter to the boy's parents. Mrs. Carlton responded, "As a mother I must protect my son's interest. Music is not just a passing fancy to him. It is indeed his whole life. My son practices a maximum of one hour per day . . . usually between two and three P.M. If an earlier or later hour would be more convenient for others, we would be happy to cooperate in any way possible."

The landlord then tried to evict the Carltons on the basis of two provisions in the lease. The first provision stated that the landlord had the right to terminate the lease upon three days' notice if he considered the tenant objectionable. The second provision stated, "No tenant shall play upon . . . any musical instrument . . . in the demised premises between the hours of eleven o'clock P.M. and the following eight o'clock A.M. if the same shall disturb or annoy other occupants of the building. No tenant shall conduct . . . instrumental practices . . . at any time."

The last sentence, which prohibited "the conducting of practice," was inconsistent with the rest of the provision, which permitted the playing of musical instruments, at least during certain hours. The court decided that if a tenant could *play* a musical instrument, he could also *practice* playing that instrument, and that the Carltons acted reasonably and within their rights when they allowed their son to play the drums for one hour a day.

Most apartment dwellers can live with an occasional pounding of drums or some similar minor disturbance. What does upset them is when the landlord fails to provide essential services such as heat or hot water, or when he allows the condition of the apartment to deteriorate.

For many years, there was little a tenant could do about such landlord failure. The law was clear: The tenant accepted the apartment "as is." There was no "warranty of habitability" that came with the lease. If the landlord refused to provide heat or to repair broken pipes, the tenant's only recourse was to try to prove that the conditions were so bad as to constitute "constructive eviction." To do this, the tenant had to show that the apartment was unfit for occupancy, and he had to move out of the apartment *before* bringing suit. If the court later decided in the landlord's favor, the tenant was legally bound to continue paying rent.

To give tenants some protection, many cities adopted special housing codes requiring landlords to provide heat, hot water, and other basic services. New York City's Housing and Maintenance Code, for example, provided that from October through May, apartments had to be kept at least 68°F. from 6:00 A.M. to 10:00 P.M. whenever the outside temperature fell below 55°F.

These regulations looked good on paper, but most large cities did not have the staff to enforce them. Even when city building inspectors issued violations, they were often ignored by the landlords. In some cases over 100 violations were issued for a single building—and still the landlords refused to take corrective action. To obtain heat, some tenants had to resort to turning on their gas stoves, creating an additional danger to health and safety.

Even when a building was poorly maintained, the landlord was able to sue his tenants to collect the rent. It was no defense for the tenant to claim that the landlord had failed to provide essential services. The right of the landlord to receive rent somehow became separate from, and superior to, the right of a tenant to live in an apartment maintained decently and in accordance with the requirements of the law.

In an article that received wide attention, two legal scholars called this situation "a scandal." This is how they described landlord-tenant law: "More often than not unjust in its preference for the cause of the landlord, it can only be described as outrageous when applied to the poor urban tenant in the multi-family dwelling. There it views with complacency the most wretched living conditions, littered and unlit hallways, stairways with steps and bannisters missing, walls and ceilings with holes, exposed wiring, broken windows, leaking pipes, stoves and refrigerators that do not work or work only now and then. And always the cockroaches, and the dread of the winter cold and uncertain heat" (Quinn and Phillips, *The Law of Landlord-Tenant; A Critical Evaluation of the Past and Guidelines for the Future*, 38 Fordham Law Review 225 (1969)).

Why has the law made it so difficult for tenants to protect their rights? The roots of the problem can probably be traced to feudal England, where a lease was considered to be primarily a conveyance or sale of land for a period of time. A tenant was expected to inspect the premises prior to the "sale," and unless there were express promises made by the landlord, the tenant took possession with whatever defects existed at the time of the lease. Of course, leases at that time were primarily for farmland, and the tenant paid the rent from the proceeds of tilling the soil. The average tenant was capable of inspecting the land for possible defects prior to entering into the lease, and if there were any physical structures, they were usually simple in design and of secondary importance. If defects arose during the term of the lease, the tenant usually had the skill and the resources to make the necessary repairs.

But times have changed. The conditions which existed in a feudal, agrarian society exist no longer, and the old doctrine of *caveat emptor,* which governed landlord-tenant relationships then, is now obsolete. One court in California explained why tenants in modern cities require greater protection:

"First, the increasing complexity of modern apartment buildings not only renders them much more difficult and expensive to repair than the living quarters of early days, but also makes adequate inspection of the premises by a prospective tenant a virtual impossibility; complex heating, electrical and plumbing systems are hidden from view, and the landlord, who has had experience with the building, is certainly in a much better position to discover and cure dilapidation in the premises. Moreover, in a multiple-unit dwelling, repair will frequently require access to equipment and areas solely in control of the landlord.

"Second, unlike the multi-skilled lessee of old, today's city dweller generally has a single, specialized skill unrelated to maintenance work. Furthermore, whereas an agrarian lessee frequently remained on a single plot of land for his entire life, today's urban tenant is more mobile than ever; a tenant's limited tenure in a specific apartment will frequently not justify efforts at expensive repairs."

Fortunately, the law is now beginning to take account of these factors. Most states, including New York, California, and Illinois, have recognized that there is an implied "warranty of habitability" in residential leases. In one recent case, the Supreme Court of New Jersey said: "In a modern society one cannot be expected to live in a multi-storied apartment building without heat, hot water, garbage disposal or elevator service. Failure to supply such things is a breach of the implied covenant of habitability."

This legal concept has been used primarily in cases involving low- and middle-income tenants, but tenants in luxury housing sometimes need protection, too. This was discovered by Mr. and Mrs. Henry Lawrence, who wanted to rent a house in the Diamond Head area of Honolulu. They found a house that seemed perfect; it faced the water, and the surrounding grounds were attractively landscaped. The property consisted of several structures containing six bedrooms, six baths, a living room, kitchen, dining room, garage, and saltwater swimming pool. The main house was constructed in "Tahitian" style with a corrugated metal roof over which coconut leaves were woven together to produce a "grass shack" effect. A real estate agent showed the house to the Lawrences and told them it was available for immediate occupancy at $800 a month. That evening they signed a lease and paid the agent a $1,190 deposit.

The next day the Lawrences and their four children moved in. But that night they were astonished to discover that there were rats within the main dwelling and on the corrugated roof. It was not clear whether the rats came from within the house or from the rocky area next to the water, but during that night—and for the next two nights—the Lawrences were sufficiently apprehensive about the rats to vacate their individual bedrooms and sleep together in the downstairs living room. After the first night, the rental agent was advised of the rats and she arranged to have a local exterminator try to alleviate the problem. The exterminator's efforts were only partially successful, however, and the next two nights were equally sleepless and uncomfortable for the Lawrence family.

The Lawrences then moved out of the house and demanded that the rental agent return the deposit. When the money was not refunded, the Lawrences filed suit. The court ruled that there had been an implied warranty of habitability and that the Lawrences were entitled to break the lease and to recover the amount paid on deposit.

In the next few years, it is likely that many states will pass new laws to protect tenants. New York State has already passed a law which provides that in "every written or oral lease or rental agreement for residential premises the landlord or lessor shall be deemed to convenant and warrant that the premises so leased or rented and all areas used in connection therewith in common with other tenants or residents are fit for human habitation and for uses reasonably intended by the parties and that occupants of such premises shall not be subjected to any conditions which would be dangerous, hazardous or detrimental to their life, health or safety."

Even if conditions in your apartment building are basically sound, you may still have problems with minor repairs. Suppose, for example, that the faucet on your sink does not work properly or the tiles on your kitchen floor become loose. Usually, your lease will provide that you have the responsibility to make such minor repairs in your apartment. The landlord, however, must repair all defects which occur in parts of the building which are not directly under your control. This means that the landlord must repair the boiler if it breaks down and fix the pipes if there is a leak in the basement. The landlord also has the responsibility to make major structural repairs. If the ceiling in your living room collapses, for example, the landlord must hire someone to make the repairs.

In many cities there are housing codes or regulations which provide that the landlord must make repairs in all parts of the building, including your apartment. So if the radiator leaks or the hinges on the door become loose, the landlord must make the repairs. In New York City and many other places, the landlord is required to paint your apartment at regular intervals.

Of course, landlords do not always bother to comply with such code provisions. What remedies do you have if your landlord refuses to make repairs despite repeated requests?

First, you can check with the housing officials in your city to see if the landlord's failure to act constitutes a violation of the city housing code. Some landlords do take action when they are notified of a violation by city inspectors.

Second, you can make the repairs yourself. If the repairs can be completed in a short time and at little cost, it may be easier to do the work yourself than to waste time arguing with your landlord. If the repair work is difficult or expensive and your landlord refuses to take any action, you can pay someone to do the work and send a bill to your landlord. If he refuses to pay, you can sue him in Small Claims Court (without a lawyer) to recover the amount of the bill.

Another possibility—and this is admittedly a more risky course to follow—is to deduct the cost of the repairs from your rent payments. In some places this procedure is specifically authorized by law, at least when the condition is dangerous or the property is dilapidated. In California a tenant may, after giving the landlord reasonable notice of "dilapidations," either leave the premises without further liability for rent or repair the dilapidations himself and deduct the cost—up to one month's rent—from his rent check.

In one New York case, a tenant notified her landlord that her toilet had ceased to function. When her landlord refused to make repairs, she hired someone at her own expense to do the job. The repairs cost the tenant $22, and she deducted this amount from her rent check. The landlord then tried to evict her for nonpayment of rent. When the case went to court, the judge sided with the tenant. He ruled that a tenant could make repairs and deduct their reasonable cost from the rent whenever (1) there was an emergency condition which seriously affected the habitability of the apartment, (2) the landlord refused to make repairs, and (3) the condition could not reasonably be permitted to continue until code-enforcement proceedings had run their course.

Keep in mind, however, that this is a risky tactic to use. Once your landlord sees that you intend to withhold all or part of your rent, he will probably sue you for the money or begin legal proceedings to have you evicted. Therefore, if you are uncertain about the law in your state, you should consult with an attorney *before* you decide to withhold rent from your landlord.

Negligence

Suppose that you live in an apartment building with three steps leading from the front door to the lobby. Some of the stones on these steps have been loose for almost a year, and your landlord has made no effort to repair them. One day, while you are walking into the building, one of the stones slips and as a result you trip and break your leg. Can you sue your landlord?

As a general rule, a landlord is required to take reasonable care to keep the premises in a safe condition. Therefore, you can sue for personal injury or property damage, but to make your case in court, you will have to establish four basic points:

1. That your landlord had a legal duty to maintain the building or make repairs and that he breached that duty.
2. That your landlord knew, or with reasonable care should have known, of the condition which caused the injury.
3. That you suffered personal injury or property damage as a result of the landlord's negligence.
4. That the injury or property damage was a reasonably foreseeable result of the landlord's negligence.

A landlord has a duty or obligation to maintain those parts of a building which are used in common by all tenants. (In most cases this includes the lobby, the hallways, the elevator, and the front steps.) Some leases have a clause stating that the landlord is not liable for personal injury or property damage in the building, but remember that in many places such clauses have been held to be unconscionable or illegal.

The tenant does not always have to show that the landlord had knowledge of the defective condition. It may be sufficient to show that the landlord, with reasonable diligence, *should* have had knowledge of the condition. When steps are broken or plaster in the ceiling of the lobby begins to fall, the landlord (or the superintendent who works for the landlord) is supposed to spot the problem and make repairs within a reasonable time.

A tenant must also be able to prove that the injury was caused by the landlord's negligence. Lawyers often put this another way: They say that there must be proof that the landlord's negligence was the *proximate cause* of the injury. This means that there must be a direct, causal relationship between the acts or omissions of the landlord and the injury. If you fall down the steps because someone pushed you, and not because the steps are in poor condition, you cannot argue that you were injured because of the landlord's negligence.

Of course, all situations are not this clear-cut. Suppose you return from work and find that a burglar has ransacked your apartment and taken all of your valuable possessions. Or suppose you are mugged in the hallway of your building. Can your landlord be held liable for the injuries that you suffer?

For many years it was generally agreed that a landlord had no duty to anticipate or provide against injuries to a tenant which were the result of criminal acts by third persons. Recently, however, the courts have begun to move in the other direction. A federal court in Washington, D.C., has ruled that where the landlord has notice of criminal occurrences in the building "and has the exclusive power to take preventive action, it does not seem unfair to place upon the landlord a duty to take those steps which are within his power to minimize the predictable risk to his tenants."

In another case, a tenant in New York City was assaulted and robbed by an assailant in the lobby of his building. The tenant claimed that for a week prior to the incident the lock on the entrance door was broken and that the landlord had removed the cylinder for repair. The tenant pointed out that the landlord had installed a bell-and-buzzer system, and had obtained a rent increase for doing this, but that the system did not work effectively because the front door was broken. There was evidence that the landlord knew about the security problem in the building because he had posted a special sign over the mailboxes:

"Notice to all tenants: There have been several robberies in the building in recent weeks due to strangers and thieves getting in through the front door. It is imperative that all tenants use the intercom system to learn who is ringing their bell before they ring back. The system was put in for your protection. . . .

"Also, when you enter the building using your own key at the lobby door, if someone or a stranger attempts to enter at the same time, please report it to the superintendent at once because a thief can gain access to the building."

At the trial, the judge found that the landlord had been negligent in maintaining the security buzzer system, but he dismissed the case on the ground that there was insufficient proof that the landlord's negligence was the cause of the tenant's injury.

This decision was reversed, however, when a higher court ruled that there was a basis for finding that the injuries resulted from the landlord's negligence. "In the instant case the landlord had actual knowledge of the criminal activities which occurred and were likely to reoccur within the building. For a monetary consideration, i.e., increased rent, the landlord assumed a duty of protection by the installation of the bell and buzzer system which was permitted to fall into disrepair. The fact that the immediate cause of the tenant's injury was the act of a third party, i.e., a criminal intruder, does not prevent the landlord's negligence from being regarded in contemplation of law as the proximate cause. . . . The landlord's neglect here gave rise to the stream of events that culminated in the tenant's injuries."

It is good news to hear that some courts are receptive to this new theory of liability. But even the prospect of winning a judgment against your landlord cannot really compensate you for the trauma of being mugged in your own apartment building. The best thing to do is to make your voice heard before you become a crime statistic. You should insist that your landlord install a lock on the outer door and maintain adequate security in the lobby and elevators of your building. If a robbery or mugging takes place, you should send written notice to your landlord and you should organize the tenants in your building to press for better security.

Subletting Your Apartment

If you have been lucky enough to find a decent apartment, you probably want to stay there at least until the end of your lease. But suppose you have to spend several months out of town on business or you decide to take a long summer vacation in Europe. You may find it helpful to sublet your apartment for the time you are away.

Your right to sublet usually depends upon the terms of your lease. Most landlords do not like to see people moving in and out of an apartment at regular intervals, and to prevent this, they insert a clause in the lease which states that the tenant cannot sublet. If your lease contains such a clause and you allow someone else to move in, your landlord may send you an eviction notice.

You should discuss these matters with your landlord before you sign your lease. If your landlord does not want to give you blanket permission to sublet, see if he will accept a provision which states: "Tenant may sublet the apartment with the written permission of the landlord, which permission shall not be unreasonably withheld." With this clause, your landlord can reject someone whom he legitimately believes will be a nuisance, but if he rejects someone without a valid reason he will be violating the terms of the lease.

If you do decide to sublet your apartment, try to give it to someone whom you know or someone who has good references. You should make it clear whether you expect rent payments to be made to you or directly to your landlord. (As the original tenant you have a legal obligation to see that the rent is paid, which means that you have to pay it yourself if the person who moves into your apartment fails to pay.) When you make arrangements to sublet, try to get a security deposit which can be used to compensate you if any damage is done to the apartment. For your own protection, you should get a written agreement, like the one below, with the person who moves in.

Agreement made this 28th day of May, 1980, between John Smith, tenant, and Thomas Jones, subtenant.

The subtenant agrees to rent Apartment 14A at 880 E. 53rd Street, New York, New York, from the tenant for the term of four months commencing June 1, 1980, and ending September 30, 1980, and to pay the amount of $450 each month to the tenant as rent. Rent payments are to be made on the first of each month.

The subtenant has on this date paid the rent for the first month and has paid a security deposit of $450. The security deposit will be returned to the subtenant after he vacates the apartment on September 30, 1980. In the event that any damage is done to the apartment or any of the personal possessions of the tenant, the tenant may deduct the cost of the repairs or the reasonable value of the property damaged from the security deposit.

The subtenant agrees to pay all utility bills including, but not limited to, electricity, gas, and telephone charged for the period June 1, 1980, to September 30, 1980. In the event that any bill is not paid, the tenant may deduct the amount of the bill from the security deposit.

The subtenant shall keep the apartment in good condition and shall clean the apartment thoroughly before vacating.

Under no circumstances shall the subtenant transfer possession of the apartment or rent the apartment to any other person or persons during said period.

John Smith
Tenant

Thomas Jones
Subtenant

You should avoid subletting your apartment to several different people who do not know one another. Otherwise, disputes may develop about such matters as who can use the stove during dinner hours, or who should pay for additional message units on the telephone bill. If the members of the group are unable to work out the problem, you may have to step in as a "neutral arbitrator." And then any decision that you make is certain to upset at least one person in the group.

Most people who sublet are interested in finding someone to take over the apartment for a short period of time. If, however, you want to move out of the apartment for good, you will want to *assign the lease*, rather than sublet. An assignment is a transfer of the right to occupy the apartment for the entire remainder of the lease. Usually, the landlord has a clause in the lease prohibiting assignment as well as subletting. If possible, then, you should obtain your landlord's permission. Even when an assignment is made, the law says that you are still responsible for the lease. If rent payments are not made, the landlord can demand the money from you. Often the easiest thing to do is to have the person who moves in sign a new lease with the landlord. This will probably benefit both you and your landlord. It will let you off the hook with your old lease and, in most cases, enable your landlord to raise the rent for the new tenant.

Eviction

You are having a heated dispute with your landlord. With a shake of his fist he threatens to lock you out of your apartment and sell your furniture to the highest bidder. Can he do it? In most states, the answer is no. A landlord cannot evict a tenant without first obtaining a court order. And usually the tenant must receive prior notice of the court hearing so that he has an opportunity to present his side of the story.

The legal procedures for eviction vary from state to state. In most states, to obtain a court order evicting a tenant the landlord must institute a special court proceeding called a *summary* or *dispossess* action. The courts usually hear such actions on an expedited basis, which means that the court may schedule a hearing within a matter of weeks.

The principal reason why a landlord may try to evict a tenant is that the tenant has failed to pay the rent. If you have not paid your rent because you are having a dispute with your landlord about the amount due, or because you just don't have the money, your landlord will probably send you a written notice demanding payment. In New York City, a landlord cannot go to court to evict a tenant for nonpayment unless he first demands payment from the tenant personally or sends the tenant a written notice. The notice will usually state that unless payment is made within three days, the landlord will take the next step in the eviction process—that is, institute a dispossess action in court to obtain a court order for your eviction.

You can usually handle landlord problems on your own, but if you receive a notice threatening eviction, you should speak to a lawyer. If you do not have the money to hire a lawyer, you may be able to get assistance from Legal Aid or Legal Services offices in your neighborhood. A lawyer will explain the procedures governing eviction in your state and will tell you whether you have a valid defense against the landlord's action. The lawyer may be able to speak to the landlord and arrange a compromise or settlement of the dispute.

If a settlement is not made, your landlord will probably serve you with formal legal papers. If this happens, do not let the papers gather dust on a shelf while you try to decide what to do. Under the law, you may have only a few days to respond to the papers. If you do not respond within the required time, your landlord may be able to obtain a *default judgment*. In other words, he may win the case by default because you have raised no defense against him.

The legal papers served by the landlord will usually state the grounds for the suit. If the action has been taken because you have failed to pay the rent, you can usually end the suit by depositing the rent payment in court, plus a small additional amount for court costs. If, however, you have decided to withhold the rent because the landlord has not furnished heat or hot water or because the landlord has not maintained the building properly, you may have a defense against the suit. If the problem is serious enough, you may want to file a *counterclaim* against your landlord for breaching the terms of the lease or breaching the "implied warranty of habitability." If the court agrees with you, it may order the landlord to pay you damages, or it may deduct the amount that you win from rent payments owed to the landlord.

Judges are very reluctant to evict tenants, especially when there is proof that a landlord has not provided essential services or complied with housing code regulations. In these cases, a judge may try to give relief to both parties. For example, the judge may order the tenant to pay rent to the landlord and at the same time order the landlord to correct all housing-code violations within 30 days.

Tenants in New York, under a special section of the Real Property Law, can defend a suit brought by a landlord by showing that there is a housing-code violation or that there is a condition which is likely to become dangerous to life, health, or safety. If the tenant presents adequate proof, the judge will "stay" the proceedings, which means that the landlord's suit to evict the tenant is placed on the back burner. The judge can then order the tenant to pay the rent to the court rather than to the landlord. The court will keep the rent payments until the landlord is able to prove that all of the necessary repairs have been made. What happens if the landlord simply refuses to do any repair work? The tenant can then apply to the court for release of some or all of the rent deposits to pay the bills for maintenance and repairs.

Termination or Renewal

If circumstances require that you leave an apartment before the expiration of the lease, bear in mind that you are responsible for the rent until the date the lease expires. Your liability is limited, however, to the actual loss of rental income suffered by the landlord as a result of your departure. If another tenant moves into the apartment, you are liable only for the time, if any, when the apartment is empty. Or if the landlord rents the apartment, but at a lower rental, you are only responsible for the difference between your rental rate and that of the new tenant.

The landlord, on the other hand, is required to make a reasonable attempt to find a replacement tenant. For this reason it is wise to notify your landlord as soon as possible, in writing, of your intention to vacate the apartment. It might also be worthwhile to look actively for a replacement yourself, by talking to friends, placing an ad in the local newspaper, and referring interested parties to the landlord.

What happens if you want to stay in your apartment beyond the expiration of the lease? That depends on the terms of the lease itself. Some leases require that you leave as soon as the lease expires; others assume that you will stay and require advance notice if you plan otherwise. Some also provide that if you stay and the landlord accepts the rent, this amounts to an automatic renewal of your lease, with the terms and conditions of the original lease continuing to apply. Read your lease carefully to find out what conditions apply in your case.

If your lease says nothing on the subject, then what happens when your lease expires depends on state law. Some statutes require that you leave; others allow you to stay, on a month-to-month basis, if your landlord has accepted any rent beyond the expiration of the lease.

A tenant in New York City who is covered by the Rent Stabilization Law has the right to renew his lease. In fact, the law provides that at least 120 days prior to the end of the tenant's lease, the landlord must send a letter to the tenant offering to renew his lease.

4

Forming a Corporation

If you are going into business, you may want to consider forming a corporation.

For many people the word "corporation" invokes an image of dour-looking men in pinstripe suits sitting around a board table discussing first-quarter earnings, or else a vast market-research department with computer consoles lining the walls. If this is your idea of a corporation, you may feel that it is too formal or complicated to suit your limited needs. Actually, a corporation need not involve hundreds of stockholders or dozens of blinking computers. A corporation can be organized by someone opening a small hardware store or starting a neighborhood newspaper delivery service. A corporation can be organized for any legitimate business purpose. Of course, if you are running an illegal bookie joint in your basement, you may not wish to file incorporation papers.

If you are starting a new business, however, you will obviously want to investigate all the possibilities, not just forming a corporation. It may be preferable to operate the business as a single proprietorship, or, if you are working with several other owners, as a partnership. Each business form has distinct advantages and disadvantages.

Single Proprietorship. If Joe Smith opens a small restaurant and puts up a sign that reads "Joe's Diner," he is operating a single proprietorship. He is simply one person operating as the sole proprietor of his own business.

This form of business may be advantageous for several reasons:
1. The owner does not have to file incorporation papers.
2. There is a minimum of government regulation.
3. The start-up costs are very low.

4. The owner is in direct control and can make business decisions without having to consult with a board of directors or
obtain approval from stockholders.

5. The owner is not subject to "double taxation," which is the
case with corporations.

There are also significant disadvantages:

1. The owner is personally liable for all debts of the business.
If creditors and suppliers cannot obtain payment from the
business, they can go after the owner's individual assets.

2. There is a lack of continuity. When the owner dies, the
business is terminated.

3. The single proprietor may find it difficult to raise capital.

Partnership. If you are setting up a business with friends or family
members, you may want to form a partnership. A partnership is
an association of two or more persons to carry on, as co-owners,
a business for profit. For example, two or three people may form
a partnership to go into the real estate business, or to open a
restaurant, cafe or pizza parlor. Rock groups sometimes form
partnerships. The individual performers (partners) agree to share
profits and expenses during the existence of the group.

To establish a partnership there must be an agreement between the partners, which can be written or oral. Usually each
partner has a right to participate in the management of the business, but the agreement may define the duties and responsibilities
of each partner. A partnership, like a single proprietorship, lacks
continuity. This means that the business terminates upon the
death or withdrawal of a partner.

Once the existence of a partnership is established, the relationship of *principal* and *agent* begins to apply. Every partner is really
an agent of the partnership and the other partners. Ordinarily,
partners are personally and individually liable for all obligations
of the partnership where the joint property is inadequate to pay
partnership debts. This can create serious problems. Assume that
you form a partnership with your cousin Willard to sell mousetraps. Willard, who is in charge of purchasing, orders 100,000
plastic parts from a supplier. The parts are delivered, but it soon
becomes clear that Willard has miscalculated. The plastic parts
cannot be used for mousetraps. The business folds and Willard
takes off for Acapulco. If funds are not available in the partnership to pay the supplier, the supplier can recover full payment
from your individual assets.

Nevertheless, many people decide to form a partnership because it is simpler than starting a corporation. Here are some of the advantages:

1. Forming a partnership is easier than forming a corporation. (Note that in some places a certificate of partnership must be filed.)
2. The start-up costs are relatively low.
3. The partners are additional sources of venture capital.
4. Compared with a single proprietorship, there is a broader management base and the work can be divided.
5. Sometimes, there are tax benefits.

And here are some of the disadvantages:

1. Partners may be personally liable for partnership debts.
2. It may be hard to find suitable partners.
3. There is a lack of continuity.
4. Authority is divided and disputes may break out between partners. If one partner believes that he has not been treated fairly, he may have to file suit to obtain an accounting from the other partners.

At some point you may have heard the expression "joint venture" and wondered what it meant. A joint venture is essentially the same as a partnership, except that it is limited in scope or duration. Theater and musical productions are sometimes considered joint ventures. And if your kids get together to open a lemonade stand, they may be engaged in a joint venture.

Corporation. A corporation is a distinct legal entity established under the authority of the state. Usually formed for the purpose of transacting business, a corporation has the power to make contracts, to sue or be sued in its own name, and to own and convey property. But the most important feature of a corporation is that, in ordinary circumstances, the stockholders are not personally liable for corporate debts or obligations. This may be the principal reason why business people choose the corporate form.

The owners of a corporation are its shareholders or stockholders—that is, all those persons who hold the shares of the corporation's stock. The number of such stockholders in a corporation can vary greatly. Some corporations have only one stockholder; American Telephone and Telegraph has three million. The responsibility for operating the corporation's business is in the hands of the corporation's officers: the president, secretary, treasurer, and vice-presidents. The officers are appointed and directed by the board of directors, and the board of directors is elected—usually on a one-share, one-vote basis—by the stockholders. It is in this way that the stockholders control the corporation. The influence or power that a single stockholder wields, however, is proportional to the number of shares held. In large corporations, the election of directors and the determination of corporate policy can be stormy affairs. In small, closely held corporations, on the other hand, control rests in the hands of a few persons who are usually in substantial agreement about the management of the business.

A corporation can offer the following advantages:

1. The stockholders have limited personal liability.
2. The corporation has continuous existence.
3. The board of directors can employ specialized management.
4. Stockholders may work for the corporation as employees and participate in pension, profit-sharing, and medical-reimbursement plans.
5. There may be tax advantages.
6. It may be easier for management to raise capital.

A corporation has the following disadvantages:

1. The charter must be approved by the state, and it is more closely regulated than the other forms of doing business.
2. It is the most expensive form of business to organize.
3. The powers of the corporation may be limited by state law or charter.
4. There is double taxation. (The corporation must pay taxes on its profits, and then the stockholders must pay taxes on income or dividends derived from the corporation.)

As noted previously, one of the principal advantages of a corporation is the fact that the stockholders are shielded from personal liability. Stockholders are not liable for any of the obligations of a corporation, and persons dealing with the corporation must look to the corporation, and not to the individual stockholders, for the payment of their claims. This is usually the case even when the stock is owned by one individual. The mere fact that one person owns all or practically all of a corporation does not subject him to personal liability for the debts of the corporation or for breach of contract by the corporation.

In rare circumstances, a court may "pierce the corporate veil" and hold individual stockholders liable. This can happen when there is proof of fraud or when there is a showing that the stockholders have not provided sufficient capital to meet the obligations of the corporation. Consider this example from a well-known case:

A pedestrian was injured in New York City when he was struck from behind by a taxicab. As a result of the accident, the pedestrian's right leg was amputated and his left leg was badly shattered. He was hospitalized for 209 days and underwent approximately twenty surgical operations.

The pedestrian filed suit against the taxicab company—a corporation. However, it was discovered that the company carried the minimum allowable insurance for taxicabs, which at that time was only $5,000. The injured party alleged that the taxicab company was dominated and controlled by two persons who had formed a hundred corporations, each having two cabs registered in the corporate name and each carrying the minimum amount of insurance. The court decided that it would be appropriate to pierce the corporation veil and allow the pedestrian to make a claim against the two individual stockholders. The court stated: "If the capital is illusory or trifling compared with the business to be done and the risks of loss, this is ground for denying the separate entity privilege."

In some states there are specific exceptions to the rule limiting stockholders' liability. In New York, for example, the ten largest stockholders of a corporation may be personally liable for all debts, wages, and salaries due to corporate employees. This is understandable, since the principals of a corporation should not be able to hide behind the corporate veil to avoid payment for services rendered by an employee. Before an employee can charge a stockholder for these services, however, he must give the stockholder written notice that he intends to hold him liable.

If you are planning to start a corporation, you should know that the principle of limited liability is not helpful in all situations. Suppliers may require a new corporation to pay in advance for all materials, since they know that the stockholders will not step forward to pay the bill if the corporation folds. Banks may refuse to lend money to a new corporation unless the stockholders or officers sign personal guarantees that they will repay the loan if the corporation defaults.

An accountant may be able to help you decide which form of business is most suited to your needs—a single proprietorship, a partnership, or a corporation. Or the accountant may be able to set up a *Subchapter S corporation*. This type of corporation is treated as a partnership for tax purposes and, in certain circumstances, can save the stockholders considerable money.

Stock Ownership

Once you have decided to start a corporation, you must answer two basic questions: Who will be issued shares in the corporation, and how much will the shares cost?

If you are working completely on your own, you will be the sole stockholder and will receive 100% of the stock issued by the corporation. However, if you are starting a business with friends or associates, you may plan to divide the stock ownership. Assume for a moment that you are starting a home-furnishings corporation with three friends. Each of the four of you is expected to receive 25% of the stock. This may seem perfect on paper, but there may be some unanticipated problems. You may have disagreements with your friends about marketing decisions, or you may not like the way the corporation distributes earnings. Since you own only 25% of the stock you may be consistently outvoted by the other stockholders. The same problems may arise if you are offered an opportunity to "buy into" an existing business. The people running the corporation may offer you a small percentage of the stock to obtain more capital, and then freeze you out of the operations. If, however, you own a majority of the stock or at least a 50% interest, you are certain to have a voice in corporate affairs.

Before forming a corporation, the organizers must decide what type of stock to issue. Basically, there are two types of stock: common and preferred. Most small corporations issue only *common stock*, the word "common" signifying that the holders of the stock are entitled to an equal pro-rata division of profit or net earnings. *Preferred stock* is a special type of stock that usually entitles the holder to receive dividends before the holders of common stock. The issuance of different kinds of stock can become fairly complicated; unless there are special factors, you will probably find it best to keep things simple by issuing only one class of common stock.

The shares of a corporation are issued in the form of stock certificates. A corporation can issue stock only in exchange for *valid consideration*—that is, the corporation must receive something of value for the stock. In most cases, stock is issued in exchange for money paid to the corporation. Many states have statutory restrictions on the kinds of consideration that can be accepted. Usually, stock can be issued for money, property, or work done—but not for work to be rendered in the future. Occasionally, the organizers of a small corporation agree to issue stock in exchange for a promise to bring business to the corporation or to provide essential trade information. This type of vague arrangement can cause problems. In one case, an inventor claimed that he was issued stock in exchange for a secret formula which he promised to transfer to the corporation. The court ruled that since he had never disclosed the formula to the corporation, he was not a bona fide stockholder. The safest procedure is to have the stockholders pay money for the shares and to make certain that full payment is received when the stock is issued.

If you are organizing a small corporation, you should determine at the outset the number of shares that the corporation will be *authorized to issue*, the number of shares that will be *actually issued*, and the *amount to be paid* for each share.

It is usually best to limit the number of authorized shares. (Many states base their initial filing fees or taxes on the number of authorized shares.) For most small corporations, 100 or 200 shares is sufficient.

The corporation does not have to issue all of the authorized shares. In fact, it is usually advisable to issue only one-third or one-half of the total. The remaining shares can be kept in reserve and issued at a later time.

How much should each share of stock cost? The answer to this question will depend on how much initial capital the corporation needs. Suppose that you have decided that the corporation needs $4,000 to begin operations. If you are going to be the sole stockholder, you can, for example, issue 100 shares at $40 per share. If four people are starting the corporation, you can issue 25 shares to each, with each stockholder paying $1,000 for his shares. Of course, you may decide that the stock should not be divided equally. One stockholder may get 50% of the stock, provided that he pays full value, which in this case would be $2,000.

A stockholder can sometimes gain a tax advantage by giving some of the money to the corporation in the form of a loan. Consider this example:

Samson decides that he will form a new corporation to sell toupees and other hairpieces. After some thought, he determines that the corporation will need at least $2,000 to begin operations.

The corporation can raise all of the required capital by issuing to Samson 100 shares of stock at $20 per share. If the corporation does well, Samson can draw out $2,000 in profits, but the money will be considered a dividend, and Samson will have to pay personal income tax on it. Suppose, however, that Samson purchases only $1,000 worth of stock and the remaining $1,000 is provided to the corporation in the form of a loan. To make matters official, a corporate officer signs a promissory note agreeing to repay the loan six months later. When the money is paid to Samson, it will be considered repayment of a loan rather than taxable income. With this arrangement, the corporation still gets the use of $2,000, and Samson avoids paying taxes on that portion considered repayment of the loan.

One note of caution: This arrangement may be scrutinized by the tax authorities if they suspect that too little money was apportioned for the payment of stock. The tax examiner may conclude that the entire amount (including the loan) should be treated as payment for shares in the corporation. In that case, all amounts subsequently paid back to the stockholder will be considered dividends and, therefore, taxable income. This type of loan arrangement should be made only after consulting an accountant. Otherwise, you may be making several "guest appearances" at the IRS office.

Before you form a corporation, you should decide whether you want to issue *par-value* stock. Par-value stock has a specific dollar value imprinted on its face. The primary purpose of par-value stock is to fix a minimum subscription price for each share. Stock *without par value* (or, as it is sometimes called, "no-par-value stock") does not have a fixed price. The shares are sold at whatever price is determined to be reasonable. Generally, there is more flexibility with no-par-value stock. Of course, in reality, the organizers of a small corporation usually decide in advance how much is going to be paid for the first shares of no-par-value stock.

California has eliminated the designation of par value and no-par-value stock, but in most states the type of stock that is going to be issued must be set forth in the articles of incorporation.

Buy and Sell Agreements

In practice, a small corporation is usually run like a partnership. The individual stockholders are active in management and help make the day-to-day business decisions. All of this can be disrupted, however, if one of the stockholders withdraws from the business or announces that he wants to sell his stock. The stockholders sometimes plan for this contingency by signing a *Buy and Sell Agreement*.

The Buy and Sell Agreement restricts the right of a stockholder to sell his shares to an "outsider" unless the corporation, or the other stockholders, are given the right of first refusal. What this means is that the corporation, or the remaining stockholders, have the right to buy the stock at a predetermined price before the shares can be sold to anyone else.

This may seem like a complicated way to resolve the problem. Why not simply prevent all of the stockholders from selling their stock? This cannot be done because a *total restraint* on the right to sell stock is invalid. However, it is usually permissible to have a limited restriction on the transfer of stock or to give the other stockholders the right of first refusal. To provide adequate notice to all parties, the restriction on the transfer of stock should be printed conspicuously on the stock certificates and in the certificate of incorporation or bylaws.

If you are organizing a small corporation, you may also be concerned about what will happen if one of the stockholders dies. A Buy and Sell Agreement usually provides that the corporation, or the surviving stockholders, can buy the shares from the estate of the deceased stockholder.

If you are preparing a Buy and Sell Agreement, you will have to decide whether the individual stockholders will be buying the shares or whether the corporation, itself, will be buying them. You will also have to decide what price will be paid for the stock. This may not be easy, because the value of the stock may rise or fall depending on how well the corporation does. To resolve this problem, the stockholders can set a price in the agreement and provide for yearly reevaluations. Sometimes this works out well, but often the stockholders get caught up in other problems and forget to make the yearly reevaluations. If this occurs, the agreement can contain a fallback provision stating that the price should be determined by the executor (or representative) of the deceased stockholder and the purchaser. If the parties cannot reach an agreement, an accountant or other third party should be called in to set a fair price.

The most difficult part of a Buy and Sell Agreement is deciding how to pay for the stock. Provision for such a circumstance is often made in advance by taking out insurance on the lives of the stockholders. When one of the stockholders dies, the proceeds of his insurance policy are used to pay for the stock.

Final Plans

Two more decisions must be made before you set up the corporation. First, you will have to decide where you are going to file the incorporation papers. Some larger firms, on the advice of counsel, decide to file in a state other than the state in which their principal business office is located because there is a particular statutory provision which benefits the corporation or the stockholders. If you are starting a small business, however, there is seldom a persuasive reason for incorporating out of state. In fact, if you file in another state, you may have to qualify as a "foreign corporation" in your home state and you may have to pay taxes and fees in two jurisdictions instead of one.

When you prepare the papers, you will also have to find a suitable name for the corporation. You cannot select a name which is already in use or which is too similar to an existing name. General Electric and Exxon are out—for obvious reasons. You will probably have to use the word "Corporation" or "Incorporated" (or an abbreviation of one of these words) in the name. Some states have a prohibition on the use of words like "bank," "finance," or "investments" because they can be misleading to the public. It is best to find a name which conveys some information about the type of product or service your corporation will offer. There is no real advantage in calling your company "Smith Corporation," unless, of course, you plan to set up shop as a blacksmith.

The filing of corporate papers is usually supervised by the secretary of state (not the one in Washington, but the one in your state capital). Before you prepare papers with the corporate name, you should call or write the secretary of state to see if the name is available. If there is a conflict with a name already in use, you may have to settle on your second or third choice. In some states it is possible to reserve the name for a limited period of time. In California the fee for reserving a corporate name is $4; in New York the fee is $10.

Even if the secretary of state approves the name, you may have legal problems if it is the same or similar to a name used by another business. On this point, you should read the information about trade names in Chapter 11 of this book.

How to File Incorporation Papers

Your first official act will be to file a *certificate of incorporation* or *charter* with the state. The certificate of incorporation should be typed on plain white paper and signed before a notary public. In most states the certificate of incorporation must contain the following information:

1. The full name of the corporation.
2. The purpose or purposes of the corporation. (It is usually best to keep the purposes as broad as possible. That way, if you expand into other areas, you will not have to file an amendment to the certificate of incorporation.)
3. The city and the county in which the office of the corporation is to be located.
4. The aggregate number of shares which the corporation is authorized to issue. If the shares are to consist of one class only, the par value of the shares or a statement that the shares are without par value; if the shares are to be divided into classes, the number of shares of each class; the designation of each class; and a statement of the relative rights, preferences, and limitations of the shares of each class.
5. The name and address in the state of the corporation's agent upon whom legal papers can be served. (In some states the corporation must designate the secretary of state as agent for the service of papers.)
6. The duration of the corporation if other than perpetual.

A sample certificate of incorporation for a New York corporation is printed at the end of this chapter. Naturally, the information required in other states may be somewhat different. You may, for example, have to disclose the names of the directors or the amount of capital invested in the corporation.

Before you prepare a certificate of incorporation, you should check the requirements with the secretary of state. You can also obtain information from the secretary of state about the fees or taxes which must be paid. (Remember that the cost of filing may be less if the corporation is planning to issue no-par-value shares or shares with a low par value.)

The persons filing the certificate of incorporation are usually referred to as the *incorporators*. In some states, like New York, the papers can be filed by only one incorporator. The usual procedure is for the incorporators to send the certificate of incorporation to the secretary of state with the filing fee. For most small corporations the fee usually runs somewhere between $50 and $200.

If the certificate of incorporation meets all of the legal requirements, the secretary of state will probably file the papers and issue a receipt. (In some cases, you may be able to obtain a certified copy of the certificate of incorporation by paying a small additional charge.) If the certificate of incorporation is not complete, the secretary of state will probably return the papers with a letter explaining what information has been omitted. You can then revise the certificate of incorporation to include this information. In most cases you will not be under any time pressure. But if you have reserved the corporate name for 30 or 60 days, you will want to be certain to file the revised certificate before the time period expires.

In some states the certificate of incorporation must also be filed in the county or city where the corporation has its principal office. Check with the secretary of state or the county clerk to make certain that you are complying with all of the filing requirements.

Organizing the Corporation

Once you have filed the certificate of incorporation, you should purchase a *corporate kit*. The kit usually contains a loose-leaf book with stock certificates, a book to keep the minutes of corporate meetings, and a stock ledger to keep a record of the stockholders. The loose-leaf book may also contain instruction sheets and sample forms for corporate minutes. In most cases you can purchase a corporate kit from a printing shop or a stationery store that sells legal supplies. The cost is usually about $25 or $30.

Most kits come with a *corporate seal*. The seal leaves a mark or impression on paper which is used to identify the corporation. You will probably need the seal when you open a corporate bank account or sign papers for a loan.

The corporate kit may also contain a set of *bylaws*. The bylaws are rules which govern the management and internal affairs of the corporation. Usually there are specific provisions in the by-laws about the number of directors, the duties and responsibilities of corporate officers, the procedures for holding meetings of the directors and stockholders, the formalities for stockholder voting (including proxies), and the procedures for issuing and transfer-ring shares.

Typical bylaws for a New York corporation are printed at the end of this chapter. Of course, other states have different rules and requirements for bylaws, so try to follow the sample forms that come in the corporate kit.

The procedures for organizing a corporation are usually deter-mined by state law. In New York the incorporators hold an or-ganization meeting to adopt the bylaws and elect directors. New York law provides that there must be at least three directors on the board. However, when a small corporation is formed with fewer than three stockholders, the number of directors can be less than three, but not less than the number of stockholders. Suppose that Mary Smith and Jane Doe decide to form a corpo-ration, each purchasing 50 shares of stock. Since the corporation will have only two stockholders, there is no requirement that there be more than two directors on the board. Mary Smith and Jane Doe can hold an organization meeting and "elect them-selves" directors of the corporation.

At the organization meeting, the incorporators usually elect a temporary secretary to keep *minutes*. The minutes form a written record of the topics discussed and voted on at a corporate meet-ing. As a practical matter, it may not be necessary for the secre-tary to take extensive notes because the parties often use the sample minutes in the corporate kit.

State law usually provides that written notices of the meeting must be given to the incorporators a certain number of days prior to the meeting. In most cases, you can move ahead with the organization meeting without this delay by having all the incor-porators sign a waiver of notice of the meeting.

In New York, the next step is to hold a meeting of the board of directors. This can usually be done on the same day as the orga-nization meeting if all the directors sign a waiver of notice of the meeting. The rules for conducting a meeting of the board of directors are set forth in the bylaws. The most important rule is that no business can be conducted at a meeting of the board unless a *quorum* is present. The bylaws usually provide that a majority of the entire board shall constitute a quorum for the transaction of business. This means that if there are five directors on the board, at least three must be present to constitute a quorum. The directors at the board meeting vote on important policy and management questions. Generally, a majority of the directors present must vote in favor of any proposal before it is passed.

At the first meeting of the board, the directors usually elect officers for the corporation, including the president, vice-president, secretary, and treasurer. The *president* is the chief executive officer of the corporation and presides at all meetings of the board of directors and stockholders. The *vice-president* fills in for the president during his absence or disability and carries out other duties and responsibilities prescribed by the board. The *secretary* keeps records for the corporation and takes minutes at all corporate meetings. Prior to each meeting of stockholders, the secretary usually prepares a certified list of stockholders entitled to vote at the meeting. The *treasurer* keeps the financial books and records of the corporation and has custody of all corporate funds and securities. In many small corporations, the directors and stockholders also serve as officers. This type of active involvement permits them to keep their eyes on the business accounts—and their hands on the money.

At the first meeting of the board, the directors decide who will receive stock in the corporation. Very often, the directors merely confirm the decisions made in advance by the organizers of the corporation. At the board meeting, the secretary presents written offers or proposals to purchase stock from the subscribers. If the offers are approved, the officers of the corporation are authorized and directed to issue the stock certificates.

The board of directors may also take the following actions:
1. Authorize the treasurer of the corporation to open a bank account.
2. Approve salaries for corporate officers.
3. Authorize the president to sign a lease for office space or to make contracts for the corporation.

In New York, the next step is to hold a meeting of the shareholders. The bylaws usually provide that notice of the meeting must be sent to each shareholder at least ten days prior to the date of the meeting. However, the meeting can be called without delay if all of the shareholders sign a waiver of notice.

The shareholders meeting cannot be convened unless there is a quorum present. When the holders of a majority of the shares entitled to vote at the meeting are present, there is a quorum. At the first meeting, the shareholders usually adopt the bylaws of the corporation and ratify all of the decisions made at the organization meeting and at the first meeting of directors.

These are the standard procedures for organizing a corporation in New York. The rules in your state may be different, so follow the instruction sheet and guidelines printed in your corporate kit. Most kits have forms for corporate bylaws and minutes which you can complete by filling in the blank spaces.

There may be a tendency to let matters slide once you have filed the certificate of incorporation. If you have to spend all of your time raising capital or searching for new business, you may want to dispense with certain "legal formalities." However, this would be a serious mistake. If you issue stock certificates without the approval of the board, or if you pay salaries to corporate officers without authorization, you may have to account to the other investors or to the tax authorities.

Professional Corporations

In recent years many doctors, lawyers, and other professionals have found it advantageous to form professional corporations to gain certain tax benefits and to participate in corporate pension and profit-sharing arrangements. (It is advisable to obtain the services of an attorney because special forms and procedures are involved.)

All fifty states have enacted statutes allowing professionals to adopt this form of business organization. In New York one or more individuals duly authorized to render the same professional service within the state may organize a professional service corporation. Here is a partial list of professionals who can incorporate in New York:

Architects
Chiropractors
Dental hygienists
Dentists
Engineers
Landscape architects
Lawyers
Nurses
Optometrists
Pharmacists

Physical therapists
Physicians, including osteopaths, with full medical licenses
Podiatrists
Public Accountants, certified and enrolled
Shorthand reporters, certified
Social workers
Veterinarians

Most states impose specific restrictions on the names that can be used by professional corporations. It would be considered inappropriate for a firm of accountants to name their corporation "Nickel and Dime, Inc." Usually, the name of a professional corporation contains the name of at least one of the individuals organizing the corporation. If John Smith forms a professional corporation to practice medicine, he will probably use the name "John Smith, M.D., Professional Corporation." Abbreviations such as "Inc." and "Ltd." are not used by professional service corporations. The usual practice is to end the corporate name with the words "Professional Corporation" or the abbreviation "P.C."

In most cases a professional corporation cannot engage in any business other than the rendering of professional services for which it was incorporated. However, the corporation is usually permitted to invest funds in real estate, mortgages, stocks, bonds, or other types of investment.

A professional corporation can render professional services only through individuals who are licensed or qualified to provide such services. For example, a professional corporation of doctors could not employ an orderly to examine patients or perform surgery.

In most states the only individuals who can be officers, directors, or stockholders of a professional corporation are persons who are authorized to practice the profession for which the corporation is formed. This is a very sensible rule. A corporation formed to practice law should not be controlled by an officer or director who is not a member of the bar.

If you are a professional, you should discuss the advantages and disadvantages of forming a professional corporation with an accountant or tax attorney. Some financial experts maintain that only a professional whose gross income exceeds $50,000 a year can benefit from forming a corporation. However, a professional should review his tax situation and retirement aims with an expert before making a decision.

As noted earlier in this chapter, one of the major reasons for forming a business corporation is that the stockholders have limited liability. Professionals, however, cannot avoid personal responsibility for their actions by incorporating. Most states now provide that every stockholder and employee of a professional corporation is personally and fully liable for any negligent and wrongful act committed by him or any person under his direct supervision while rendering professional services on behalf of the corporation.

There may be some practical disadvantages to incorporation. The organizers of a professional corporation will have to keep a separate set of books and records, and there will be more forms to complete. The fees for legal and accounting services will probably be more, especially during the first year that the corporation is in existence. There may also be state laws restricting the right to transfer shares in the corporation. In New York, a stockholder of a professional corporation may not sell or transfer his shares except to an individual who is licensed to practice the same profession.

Even when a professional is able to sell his stock, he may find it difficult to sever his affiliation with the corporation. In one recent case, a podiatrist named Leonard McCoy formed a New York professional corporation under the name "Leonard McCoy, D.P.M., P.C." The doctor then decided to move to Florida and sold all of his stock in the corporation to two podiatrists. Several years later they in turn sold the stock to two other podiatrists. The new owners continued the practice under the name "Leonard McCoy, D.P.M., P.C." even after they received a notice from Dr. McCoy objecting to the use of that name. Dr. McCoy then filed suit requesting an injunction against the continued use of the name. The question which the court had to consider was: Can there by a Leonard McCoy, D.P.M., P.C. without a Leonard McCoy? The judge decided that the continued use of the name violated public policy and he issued an injunction restraining the defendants from using the name.

SAMPLE FORM

CERTIFICATE OF INCORPORATION FOR A NEW YORK CORPORATION

WE, THE UNDERSIGNED, natural persons of the age of eighteen years or more, acting as incorporators of a corporation under Section 402 of the Business Corporation Law, hereby adopt the following Certificate of Incorporation for such corporation:

FIRST: the name of the corporation is

* * * INC.

SECOND: the purposes for which the corporation is formed are:

To engage in the business of manufacturing, making, creating, developing, owning, acquiring, processing, shipping, storing, using, exhibiting, distributing, buying, selling, marketing, importing, exporting and generally dealing in and with clothing, wearing apparel, coats, undergarments, jackets, garments, shirts, sweaters, blouses, slacks, pants, suits, dresses, skirts, belts, pocket-books, wallets, leather goods, jewelry and accessories.

The powers, rights and privileges provided in this certificate of incorporation are not to be deemed in limitation of other or additional powers, rights and privileges granted or permitted to a corporation by the Business Corporation Law, it being intended that this corporation shall have all the rights, powers and privileges granted or permitted to a corporation by such statute.

THIRD: The office of the corporation is to be located in the City of New York, County of New York, State of New York.

FOURTH: The corporation is authorized to issue only one class of stock. The total number of shares that the corporation is authorized to issue is two hundred shares. Each share shall be without par value.

FIFTH: The Secretary of State of the State of New York is designated agent of the corporation on whom process against it may be served. The Secretary of State shall mail a copy of any process against the corporation served on him to:

> [insert name of corporation]
> 910 E. 53rd Street
> New York, New York 10026

SIXTH: The accounting period which the corporation intends to establish as its first fiscal year for reporting the franchise tax on business corporations shall begin on July 1, 1979 and end on June 30, 1980.

IN WITNESS WHEREOF, we have made and subscribed this certificate this 1st day of July, 1979.

MARY SMITH	JANE DOE
914 E. 62nd Street	982 E. 70th Street
New York, New York	New York, New York

STATE OF NEW YORK   } ss.:
COUNTY OF NEW YORK }

On this 1st day of July, 1979, before me personally came Mary Smith and Jane Doe, to me known and known to me to be the persons described in and who executed the foregoing Certificate of Incorporation and they duly acknowledged to me that they executed the same.

NOTARY PUBLIC

BYLAWS
of
____ * * * * * ____ , INC.

ARTICLE I—OFFICES. The principal office of the corporation shall be in the City, County, and State of New York. The corporation may also have offices at such other places within or without the State of New York as the business of the corporation may require.

ARTICLE II—SHAREHOLDERS' MEETINGS.

1. *Place of Meetings.* Meetings of shareholders shall be held at the principal office of the corporation or at such place as the board shall authorize.

2. *Annual Meetings.* The annual meeting of the shareholders shall be held on the 10th day of January at 10:00 A.M. in each year.

3. *Special Meetings.* Special meetings of shareholders may be called at any time by the board of directors or by the president and shall be called by the president or the secretary at the request in writing of a majority of the board or at the request in writing by shareholders owning a majority in amount of the shares issued and outstanding. Such request shall state the purpose or purposes of the proposed meeting. The written notice of the meeting shall be given not less than 10 nor more than 50 days before the meeting. No business other than that specified in the notice of meeting shall be transacted at said meeting.

4. *Record Date.* For the purpose of determining the shareholders entitled to notice of or to vote at any meeting of shareholders or any adjournment thereof, or for the purpose of any other action, the board shall fix, in advance, a date as the record date for any such determination of shareholders. Such date shall not be more than 50 nor less than 10 days before the date of such meeting, nor more than 50 days prior to any other action.

5. *Quorum.* The holders of a majority of the shares entitled to vote thereat shall be necessary to constitute a quorum at a meeting of shareholders for the transaction of any business.*

---

* The Certificate of Incorporation may provide for a quorum of more than a majority.

If a quorum shall not be present, the shareholders present may adjourn the meeting to a future date.

6. *Waivers*. Notice of meeting need not be given to any shareholder who signs a waiver of notice before or after the meeting. Attendance by any shareholder at a meeting, without protesting prior to the conclusion of the meeting the lack of notice of such meeting, shall constitute a waiver of notice by him.

7. *Proxies*. Every shareholder entitled to vote at a meeting of shareholders may authorize another person or persons to act for him by proxy.

Every proxy must be dated and signed by the shareholder or by his attorney-in-fact. No proxy shall be valid after the expiration of eleven months from the date of its execution unless otherwise provided in the proxy. Every proxy shall be revocable at the pleasure of the shareholder executing it, except as otherwise provided by law.

8. *Voting*. Every shareholder shall be entitled to one vote for each share standing in his name on the record of shareholders. The directors of the corporation shall be elected by a plurality of the votes cast at a meeting of shareholders by the holders of shares entitled to vote in the election. All other corporate action shall be authorized by a majority of the votes cast.

9. *Consents*. An action that may be taken by vote may be taken without a meeting on written consent, setting forth the action so taken, signed by the holders of all the outstanding shares entitled to vote.

ARTICLE III—DIRECTORS

1. *Board of Directors*. The business of the corporation shall be managed by its board of directors. Each director shall be at least 18 years of age.

2. *Number of Directors*. The number of directors constituting the entire board shall be three. When all of the shares are owned by less than three shareholders, the number of directors may be less than three, but not less than the number of shareholders.

3. *Election and Term of Directors*. At each annual meeting of shareholders, directors shall be elected to hold office until the next annual meeting. Each director shall hold office until the expiration of the term for which he is elected, and until his successor has been elected and qualified.

4. *Newly Created Directorships and Vacancies*. Newly created directorships resulting from an increase in the number of directors

and vacancies occurring in the board of directors for any reason except the removal of directors without cause may be filled by a vote of a majority of the directors then in office, although less than a quorum exists. Vacancies occurring in the board by reason of the removal of directors without cause shall be filled only by vote of the shareholders. A director elected to fill a vacancy shall be elected to hold office for the unexpired term of his predecessor.

5. *Removal of Directors.* Any or all of the directors may be removed for cause by vote of the shareholders, or by action of the board. Directors may be removed without cause only by vote of the shareholders.

6. *Resignation.* A director may resign at any time. Such resignation shall be made in writing and, unless otherwise specified in the notice, shall take effect upon receipt thereof by the board or by the president or the secretary. The acceptance of the resignation shall not be necessary to make it effective.

7. *Quorum of Directors.* Unless otherwise provided in the certificate of incorporation, a majority of the entire board shall constitute a quorum for the transaction of business or of any specified item of business.

The vote of a majority of the directors present at the time of the vote, if a quorum is present at such time, shall be the act of the board.

8. *Place and Time of Board Meetings.* The board of directors may hold its meetings at the office of the corporation or at such other places as it may from time to time determine.

9. *Annual Meetings.* An annual meeting of the board shall be held immediately following the annual meeting of shareholders at the place of such annual meeting of shareholders.

10. *Notice of Meetings of the Board.*

(a) Regular meetings of the board may be held without notice at such time and place as the board shall determine.

(b) Special meetings of the board shall be held upon notice to the directors and may be called by the president upon 10 days notice to each director either personally or by mail or by wire. Notice of a meeting need not be given to any director who submits a signed waiver of notice whether before or after the meeting or who attends the meeting without protesting prior thereto or at its commencement, the lack of notice to him.

(c) A majority of the directors present, whether or not a quorum is present, may adjourn any meeting to another time and place. Notice of an adjournment shall be given all directors who were not present at the time of the adjournment and, unless such time and place are announced at the meeting, to the other directors.

11. *Executive and Other Committees.* The board, by resolution adopted by a majority of the entire board, may designate from among its members an executive committee and other committees, each consisting of three or more directors. Each such committee shall serve at the pleasure of the board of directors.

12. *Compensation.* No compensation shall be paid to directors, as such, for their services to the corporation, but by resolution of the board a fixed sum and expenses may be authorized for attendance at each regular or special meeting of the board. Nothing herein contained shall be construed to preclude any director from serving the corporation in any other capacity and receiving compensation therefor.

ARTICLE IV—OFFICERS

1. *Offices.* The board may elect or appoint a president, one or more vice-presidents, a secretary and a treasurer, and such other officers as it may determine.

2. *Election.* All officers shall be elected or appointed to hold office until the meeting of the board following the next annual meeting of shareholders.

3. *Term of Office.* Each officer shall hold office for the term for which he is elected or appointed, and until his successor has been elected or appointed and qualified.

4. *Removal of Officers.* Any officer elected or appointed by the board may be removed by the board with or without cause.

5. *Duties of Officers.* The duties and powers of the officers of the corporation shall be as follows:

PRESIDENT.

A. The president shall be the chief executive officer of the corporation;

B. The president shall preside at all meetings of the board of directors and shareholders;

C. The president shall supervise and manage the business affairs of the corporation; and

D. The president shall see that all orders and resolutions of the board are carried into effect and shall enforce all of the provisions of these bylaws.

VICE-PRESIDENT.

During the absence or incapacity of the president, the vice-president shall have all the powers and perform all the duties of the president. The vice-president shall perform such duties and functions as the board shall prescribe.

SECRETARY.

A. The secretary shall attend all meetings of the board of directors and of the shareholders and record all votes and minutes of all proceedings in a book kept for that purpose;

B. The secretary shall give or cause to be given notice of all special meetings of the board of directors and of all meetings of the shareholders;

C. The secretary shall be custodian of the records of the corporation and affix the seal to any instrument when authorized by the board;

D. The secretary shall prepare and make available at each meeting of shareholders a certified list in alphabetical order of the names of shareholders entitled to vote at the meeting, indicating the number of shares of each respective class held by each;

E. The secretary shall perform such other duties as are assigned to him by the board of directors.

TREASURER.

A. The treasurer shall have the care and custody of the funds and securities of the corporation;

B. The treasurer shall keep full and accurate accounts of receipts and disbursements in the corporate books;

C. The treasurer shall deposit all money and other valuables in the name and to the credit of the corporation in such depositories as may be designated by the board;

D. The treasurer shall disburse the funds of the corporation in such manner as may be ordered or authorized by the board;

E. The treasurer shall report the condition of the finances of the corporation at each regular meeting of the board of directors and render a full financial report at the annual meeting of the shareholders;

F. The treasurer shall perform such other duties as are assigned to him by the board of directors.

ARTICLE V—CERTIFICATES FOR SHARES

1. *Certificates*. The shares of the corporation shall be represented by certificates and shall be signed by the president or a vice-president and the treasurer or the secretary and shall bear the corporate seal. The certificates shall be numbered consecutively and in the order in which they are issued. Each certificate shall state the registered holder's name, the number of shares and the date of issue.

2. *Subscriptions*. Subscriptions to the shares shall be paid at such time and in such installments as the Board of Directors may determine.

3. *Lost or Destroyed Certificates*. The board may direct a new certificate or certificates to be issued in place of any certificate or certificates issued by the corporation, alleged to have been lost or destroyed, upon the making of an affidavit of that fact by the person claiming their certificate to be lost or destroyed. When authorizing such issue of a new certificate or certificates, the board may, in its discretion, require the owner of such lost or destroyed certificate or certificates, or his legal representative, to give the corporation a bond in such sum and with such surety sufficient to indemnify the corporation against any claim that may be made against the corporation on account of the certificate alleged to have been lost or destroyed.

4. *Transfer of Shares*. The shares of the corporation shall be assignable and transferable only on the books and records of the corporation by the owner, or his attorney, upon surrender of the certificate for shares duly endorsed with proper evidence of authority to transfer. Every transfer shall be entered on the transfer book of the corporation. No transfer shall be made within 10 days next preceding the annual meeting of shareholders.

ARTICLE VI—DIVIDENDS

The Board of Directors may declare dividends on the outstanding shares of the corporation payable out of the surplus of the corporation. The dividends may be paid in cash, property or shares of the corporation.

ARTICLE VII—CORPORATE SEAL

The seal of the corporation shall be circular in form and have inscribed thereon the name of the corporation, the year of its organization and the words "Corporate Seal" and "New York." The seal may be used by causing it or a facsimile to be affixed or impressed or reproduced in any manner.

ARTICLE VIII—EXECUTION OF INSTRUMENTS

All corporate instruments and documents shall be signed, executed, or acknowledged by such officer or officers or other person or persons as the board may designate.

ARTICLE IX—FISCAL YEAR

The fiscal year shall begin on the first day of July in each year.

ARTICLE X—CHANGES IN THE BYLAWS

Bylaws may be adopted, amended or repealed by vote of the holders of the shares entitled to vote in the election of any directors. The Bylaws may be adopted, amended, or repealed by the Board of Directors, but any Bylaw adopted by the board may be amended or repealed by the shareholders entitled to vote in the election of any directors.

Regulation and Licensing for Small Business

Every business, no matter how small, is required nowadays to operate under the constraints and requirements of a whole host of governmental licensing and regulatory agencies. The requirements vary from place to place and from one kind of business to another, but what follows is a listing of the general areas of concern. As a rule, if you intend to go into business you should contact all the government agencies—whether federal, state, county, or local—that might have something to say about how you conduct your business.

This might require a little persistence, but it is important that you find out before you begin what is going to be required of you. If time is at all important—and it seldom is not important—then you will want to pursue this by telephone rather than by mail. Often a request by mail for such information will result in a return of your letter with instructions to send it to some other address or some other agency, with a considerable loss of time. If you phone, however, you may have to talk to a number of people—who will switch you from person to person to person—but eventually, with persistence, you will talk to the right department or agency. Explain what you intend to do and request a copy of any applicable laws or regulations. You will, of course, have to talk to a number of different agencies, because more than one set of laws or regulations will be involved.

Business Certificate

One of your first concerns will be to establish a name for your business and to register that name with the county in which your business will be located. Do not make the mistake of assuming that you will be able to register whatever name you choose and simply go ahead and begin to conduct business in that name, signing leases and ordering signs, labels, stationery, etc., with the intention of registering the name later. When you finally get around to registering your name, you just may discover that someone else is already using it, in which case you will have to come up with a new name, and new stationery.

After choosing the name you want to use, check with your county clerk's office to find out whether or not that name is available. If it is, you should then fill out a number of copies of a Business Certificate form (which may be purchased at any well-equipped stationery store that sells legal forms) and have them approved and certified by the county. In order to open a checking account in your company's name, the bank may require a copy of your Business Certificate. The same is true of the post office if you intend to have a post-office box in your business' name.

If you are going to incorporate your business, this procedure of registering your business' name will not be required, because that is taken care of through the incorporation process.

Licenses

Many kinds of businesses require a special license from either the city or state in which they are located. Depending on the location, some of the businesses requiring special licenses are: real estate brokers, barbers, contractors, hairdressers, private investigators, cosmetologists, pool rooms, newsstands, locksmiths, dry cleaners, liquor stores, service stations, grocery stores, employment agencies, sidewalk cafes, restaurants, bars, and street peddlers. For years New York City even licensed miniature golf courses.

Be certain to check with both city and state licensing agencies. You will be required to fill out an application, usually pay a fee, and sometimes take a test, depending on the kind of business, before you will be granted a license.

There is probably little to be gained by complaining about the fee you will have to pay. A licensing authority has the right to charge a reasonable fee to compensate for the expense of issuing and recording the license and regulating the business practices. In fact, complaints in this area usually fall under the heading of "fighting City Hall." However, one license holder—a plumber—managed to make some headway when he tried to recover the excess amount paid on renewal of his license. He asked a court to allow him to file a class action to recover the overpayment. The court granted his application to proceed on behalf of the class, since approximately 1,200 other people were eligible to receive the same relief.

The application for a license may request information about financing or capital structure, previous experience, number of employees, etc. Some licensing agencies also inquire about criminal records and will refuse to grant a license to an applicant with a conviction. In other situations, an agency may try to deny the license on the ground that the applicant does not have "good moral character." New York State, though, has passed a law that provides that no agency can deny an application for a license because the applicant has been convicted of a criminal offense or because there has been a finding of "lack of good moral character," unless (1) there is a direct relationship between the criminal offense and the specific license sought, or (2) the issuance of the license would involve an unreasonable risk to property or the safety or welfare of the general public.

When you call or apply for information about a license, try to learn as much as possible about the specific requirements imposed by the agency. It may be necessary, for example, to renew the license at periodic intervals or to take regular examinations to demonstrate competency in the particular field in which you are working. The agency may even require you to use a standard form of contract or invoice and to keep records of all of your transactions with customers.

Sales Taxes

Most states and large cities now have sales taxes. This places a responsibility on the small business for collecting such taxes from customers at the time the sale is made and passing them on periodically, usually quarterly, to the appropriate government agency. You will need to contact both state and local agencies to determine which goods and services require the collection of sales taxes and how this is done. Usually, you will have to fill out another application, after which you will be assigned a sales tax reference number for your particular business establishment and given the appropriate forms and instructions for transmitting the sales taxes to the city or state, or both.

Employees

If you will have one or more employees working in your business, you will have to contact a number of federal, state, and city agencies regarding employee matters.

You will need to contact your state's department of labor regarding labor regulations, such as working hours, minimum wages, working conditions, the hiring of minors, etc. Your state's department of labor will also advise you about such matters as unemployment insurance and workmen's compensation.

As an employer you will have to collect income taxes and contributions to social security. Contact your local Internal Revenue Service office for an application for an employer identification number. Also, for information about federal tax withholding and reporting requirements, ask for IRS Publication 539. If your state has an income tax, contact your state's department of taxation. The same is true if your city has an income tax; contact the city for the necessary forms and instructions.

Health Regulations

A number of businesses require adherence to public health laws and sanitary codes. This is particularly true of all businesses which process and dispense food and/or drink to the public. This would include food processors, such as dairies, soda bottlers, bakeries, and confectioners, as well as grocery stores, street vendors, restaurants, and bars. Contact your local department of health for a copy of all health regulations applicable to your business. It is important that you get this information early in the formation of your business, since if you are going to open a restaurant, for example, the regulations may affect the kind of equipment you will need (such as dishwashing machines), restroom facilities, food-handling procedures, employee sanitation, and pest control.

Other businesses which involve customer health and which may be affected by health regulations include barber shops, hairdressers, cosmetologists, and massage parlors.

If your business does not measure up to local health codes and regulations, a surprise inspection may result in the closing of your business, and loss of income, until the deficiencies are corrected.

Building, Fire, and Zoning Codes

Most communities, of whatever size, have now adopted codes which regulate the uses of buildings and property located in various areas, or zones, in the community. Such zoning codes describe which areas are available for commercial and/or manufacturing use, and which are reserved exclusively for residential use. Make certain that local zoning codes permit you to conduct your kind of business at the location you intend. If your interest in cars has led you to consider opening an auto repair shop in your garage, you may discover that such a business is not permitted in your residential area.

It is also important that the building you are going to use for your business conform to local building and fire codes. If you are going to do extensive remodeling of your building before opening for business, you will probably have to have your remodeling plans approved by the local building department. And once the work is completed it will need to be inspected and approved before you are issued a Certificate of Occupancy. By the time you are ready to move in, the building will have to conform to all sorts of requirements having to do with the electricity and plumbing, lighting, building materials, heating and ventilation, emergency exits, fire extinguishers, sprinkler systems, etc., depending upon the details of your particular business and the building in which you will conduct it.

Miscellaneous

The regulation of business seems to know no bounds. In addition to what we have touched on in this chapter, there are also regulations having to do with the issuance of credit; the pollution of air, water, and land; the disposal of solid waste; the days of the week and hours of the day when business can be conducted; the use of chemicals; packaging; advertising claims; prices; and so on.

If you fail to obtain a license or you consistently flout the regulations of a governmental agency, the agency may take you to court or may subpoena your books and records. Not only may you be getting into hot water with the government, but you may be jeopardizing your right to obtain payment from your customers. Consider this case:

A home-improvement contractor from Queens, New York, did some contruction work for private homeowners, although he was not licensed as required by the Administrative Code of the City of New York. When the homeowners failed to pay for the work, he took them to court. The contractor explained that he had entered into an oral agreement to build a patio in the back of the house, and since the work had to be done right away, he and two employees had to work during Memorial Day. But the court rejected his claim, stating:

"It is the purpose of the City Council in enacting [a licensing provision] to safeguard and protect the homeowner against abuses and fraudulent practices by licensing persons engaged in the home improvement, remodeling and repair business.

"The court finds that this statute was enacted for the very purpose of protecting homeowners such as defendants, and, accordingly, a contract made for a home improvement by an unlicensed contractor, such as plaintiff, is unenforceable."

Every line of business must deal with its own unique combination of rules and regulations. Consequently, one of the best sources of information about any particular line of business is the trade association that has been organized by those people who are already in that business. If you want to open a restaurant, for example, it may be well to contact the National Restaurant Association. The association may have literature available that would be helpful to you, or may have a trade magazine to which you could subscribe that would give you a good view of the special problems and concerns of the restaurant business.

Franchises

Franchising is a method of doing business that has expanded greatly in the United States in recent years. Typically, a franchise operation comes into existence when someone develops a successful small-business formula and then, for a fee and royalties, gives others the right to use that formula, which usually includes the product, name, trademark, and sales and distribution techniques. This is really a licensing arrangement in which the franchisor grants a license to the franchisee.

For those contemplating the purchase of a franchise, the most important—and sometimes the most difficult—thing to do is to get all the information from the franchisor that they need to make an intelligent decision. To aid the prospective investor, the Federal Trade Commission has recently issued regulations requiring that certain important information be provided by all franchisors to those exploring the purchase of a franchise. The regulations require not only disclosure of information about the business experience and background of the officers and managers of the franchisor, but precise details about the nature of the relationship with the franchisee. This will include information regarding fees, royalties, inventory and equipment purchases, management assistance, and any other conditions existing between the franchisor and franchisee. The FTC rules also prohibit franchisors from making unrealistic and misleading claims about a franchisee's prospects for sales and profits. (You may obtain a copy of the "Franchise Rule" by writing to the Federal Trade Commission, Sixth and Pennsylvania Avenue N.W., Washington, D.C. 20580.)

If you decide to purchase a franchise, you will have to enter into a contract with the franchisor. It is important that you go over the contract very carefully and that you discuss with the franchisor any aspects of the contract that are unclear to you. Follow closely the advice in Chapter 2 on contracts. Reading that chapter will impress you with the importance of the contract and the need to "get it in writing." If there is some aspect of the contract that is not acceptable to you, have the franchisor change it. Do not accept any oral agreements or promises. If the franchisor makes any promise or representation to you that is not specifically covered in the contract, insist on its being added to the contract. Taking the time to go over the fine print at the outset could help you avoid a lot of difficulty later.

Remember, however, that the authority to operate a franchise business does not in any way modify your responsibility to abide by the entire range of local, state and federal regulations. The franchise agreement pertains only to the relationship between you and the franchisor. You must still be a regulation-abiding businessperson in all respects.

6

Divorce

There has been such a sharp increase in the number of divorces in recent years that today divorce seems almost as common as marriage. According to the National Center for Health Statistics, more than one million divorces are granted in this country every year. Most of these are still handled by lawyers. But the secret is now out that it is possible to get a divorce without a lawyer.

It is important to note at the outset that there are times when you should definitely be represented by a lawyer. If your spouse does not want to end the relationship and plans to contest the divorce in court, if you have children and there is a dispute about who will have custody, or if there is a house or other substantial assets that will have to be divided, you should retain the services of a lawyer. A lawyer who is familiar with the laws and legal precedents in your state will be able to marshal all the facts and present them to the court in the manner most effective for the protection of your interests.

This chapter, however, is intended to assist those couples who want a simple "noncontested" divorce—that is, a divorce in which both parties want the divorce and there is no substantial conflict about child custody or about money matters. For handling such divorces, attorneys in private practice charge from $300 to $1,000, depending on locality, even though in some cases they only have to complete a few forms and make a token appearance in court. You can, however, usually get such a divorce without a lawyer, and this chapter is designed to help you do so.

Grounds for Divorce

If you have decided to file for a divorce, you must first make certain that you have legal grounds. Most couples usually decide to get a divorce because they are no longer compatible. But except in a few states, such as Connecticut and Nevada, "incompatibility" is not recognized as a valid ground for divorce. In many jurisdictions, a divorce will not be granted simply because the marriage has not developed into a happy one or because the husband and wife are not able to get along well together.

The specific grounds for divorce vary from state to state. The charts on pages 78–79 list the grounds in each state.

Adultery is generally recognized as a ground for divorce in most jurisdictions. In fact, until 1967 adultery was the only ground for divorce in New York State.

Adultery is usually defined as an act of voluntary sexual intercourse by a married person with someone other than his or her spouse. Some time ago a judge was asked to determine whether the definition of adultery in New York State included sodomy. The judge ruled that it did not, and so the state legislature amended the statute. Now an action for divorce can be maintained in New York whenever there is proof of an act of sexual intercourse or an act of *deviate* sexual intercourse with someone other than the spouse.

How do you prove adultery? Most people assume, incorrectly, that the only way to prove adultery is to catch the husband or wife in bed with someone else. Or they think that it is necessary to hire a private investigator to take incriminating pictures. Of course, you can build a solid case on the basis of direct evidence or eyewitness accounts, but in many instances it is possible to prove adultery by circumstantial evidence. This is done by showing that your spouse had the "inclination" and the "opportunity."

Suppose you can prove that on several occasions your husband stayed overnight in a motel room with another woman. This type of circumstantial evidence will usually give rise to an inference that adultery has been committed. The guilty parties can try to furnish an explanation for the court—but what plausible story can the couple come up with? That they were watching a series of foreign films on late-night television?

Adultery is not a very popular ground for divorce because most people do not like to air their dirty linen in public. If one of the marriage partners sues for divorce on the basis of adultery, the other often feels compelled to fight the case in court.

There are legal defenses to adultery which are recognized in most states. The first of these is *connivance*, which is defined as consent or permission by one spouse for an act of adultery by the other. This is not common, but it does happen. For example, suppose that a husband and his wife decide to go to a party where they know that there will be an opportunity to swap partners. The husband cannot encourage the wife to go into a bedroom with someone else at the party and then expect to win a divorce on the basis of adultery.

Another defense which can be raised is *condonation*. A person who is charged with adultery can claim that the spouse condoned or excused the behavior. Let's say that you know that your wife is having an affair with another man. If your wife breaks off the affair and you decide to resume living together, you have condoned her misconduct. The court will probably not grant a divorce for adultery unless she goes back to her lover or starts a new relationship with someone else.

There is another defense called *recrimination*, which works like this: The person charged with adultery turns around and accuses the other of the same offense. Many states have a requirement that the person filing for divorce on the ground of adultery must be innocent of any wrongdoing. If there is proof that only the defendant committed adultery, a divorce will be granted. But if the court finds that both parties committed adultery, neither one will be granted a divorce.

What is the point of keeping two people together under these conditions? One judge suggested that under such circumstances the parties might live together and find sources of forgiveness "in the humiliation of mutual guilt."

The doctrine of recrimination has been criticized by many legal commentators. Henry Foster and Doris Freed, two experts in the field of divorce law, have pointed out that the "vice of the doctrine of recrimination . . . is that it ignores reality by assuming that all the fault is on one side and all the innocence on the other in marital failures, that two wrongs make it right that a divorce be denied, and that the parties will get back together again" (Foster and Freed, *Law and the Family*, p. 395).

To soften the harsh effects of this doctrine, some states have

DIVORCE LAWS AS OF DECEMBER 31, 1977*

State or other jurisdiction	Residence required before filing suit for divorce	"No fault" divorce(a) Marriage breakdown (b)	Separation	Prior decree of limited divorce	Adultery	Mental and/or physical cruelty	Desertion	Alcoholism and/or drug addiction	Impotency
Alabama	6 mos.(c)	•	2 yrs.(d)	2 yrs.	•	...	1 yr.	•	•
Alaska	...	•	...	...	•	•	1 yr.	•	•
Arizona	90 days	•	...	...	...	...	...	...	...
Arkansas	60 days(g)	...	3 yrs.	...	•	•	1 yr.	•	•
California	(i)	•	...	...	...	...	...	...	...
Colorado	90 days	•	...	...	...	...	...	...	...
Connecticut	1 yr.(k)	•	18 mos.	...	•	•	1 yr.	•	...
Delaware	3 mos.	•	...	...	•	•	•	...	...
Florida	6 mos.	•	...	...	...	...	...	...	...
Georgia	6 mos.	•	...	...	•	•	1 yr.	•	•
Hawaii	3 mos.	•	2 yrs.(d)	•(q)	...	...	...	...	...
Idaho	6 wks.	•	5 yrs.	...	•	•	•	•	•
Illinois	90 days	...	...	...	•	•	1 yr.	2 yrs.	•
Indiana	6 mos.	•	...	...	...	...	...	...	•
Iowa	1 yr.	•	...	...	...	...	...	...	...
Kansas	60 days	•	...	...	•	•	1 yr.	•	•
Kentucky	180 days(t)	•	...	...	...	...	...	...	...
Louisiana	(u)	...	2 yrs.	•(v)	•	•	...	...	...
Maine	6 mos.(k)	•	...	...	•	•	3 yrs.	•	•
Maryland	(x)	...	(y)	...	•	...	1 yr.	•	•
Massachusetts	30 days	•	...	...	•	•	1 yr.	•	•
Michigan	180 days(k)	•	...	...	...	...	...	...	...
Minnesota	1 yr.(k)	•	...	...	...	...	...	...	...
Mississippi	1 yr.	•	...	...	•	•	1 yr.	•	•
Missouri	90 days	•	...	...	...	...	...	...	...
Montana	90 days	•	...	...	...	...	...	...	...
Nebraska	1 yr.	•	...	...	...	...	...	...	...
Nevada	6 wks.(k)	•	1 yr.(p)	...	...	...	...	...	...
New Hampshire	1 yr.(k)	•	...	...	•	•	2 yrs.	•	•
New Jersey	1 yr.	...	18 mos.	...	•	•	1 yr.	•	•
New Mexico	6 mos.	•	...	...	•	•	...	...	...
New York	1 yr.(k)	...	1 yr.(d)	...	•	•	1 yr.	...	...
North Carolina	6 mos.	...	1 yr.	...	•	...	...	...	(af)
North Dakota	1 yr.	•	...	1 yr.	•	•	1 yr.	•	•
Ohio	6 mos.	•(ah)	2 yrs.	...	•	•	1 yr.	•	•
Oklahoma	6 mos.(aj)	•	...	...	•	•	1 yr.	•	•
Oregon	6 mos.	•	...	...	...	...	...	...	...
Pennsylvania	1 yr.	...	...	...	•	•	2 yrs.	...	•
Rhode Island	2 yrs.	...	5 yrs.(p)	...	•	•	5 yrs.(am)	•	•
South Carolina	3 mos.(ap)	...	3 yrs.	...	•	•	1 yr.	•	...
South Dakota	...	...	...	...	•	•	1 yr.	•	•
Tennessee	6 mos.	...	...	2 yrs.(p)	•	•	1 yr.	•	•
Texas	6 mos.	•	3 yrs.	...	•	•	1 yr.	•	...
Utah	3 mos.	...	3 yrs.(d)	...	•	•	1 yr.	•	•
Vermont	6 mos.(as)	...	6 mos.	...	...	•	•	...	...
Virginia	6 mos.	...	1 yr.	(at)	•	•	1 yr.	...	...
Washington	...	•	...	...	...	...	...	...	...
West Virginia	1 yr.(k)	...	2 yrs.	...	•	•	1 yr.	•	...
Wisconsin	6 mos.	...	1 yr.	1 yr.	•	•	1 yr.	1 yr.	...
Wyoming	60 days(k)	...	2 yrs.(au)	...	•	•	1 yr.	•	•
Dist. of Col.	6 mos.	...	6 mos.(ax)	•(ay)	...	...	...	...	...
Puerto Rico	1 yr.(k)	...	2 yrs.	...	•	•	1 yr.	•	•

*Prepared by the Women's Bureau, U.S. Department of Labor, with the assistance of the attorneys general of the states.

(a) "No fault" includes all proceedings where it is not necessary to prove one of the traditional grounds for divorce. Not all states shown in this category refer to their proceedings as "no fault."

(b) Expressed in statutes as irremediable or irretrievable breakdown of marriage relationship, irreconcilable differences, incompatability, marriage unsupportable because of discord, etc.

(c) Two years for wife filing on ground of nonsupport.

(d) Under decree of separate maintenance and/or written separation agreement.

(e) Crime against nature.

(f) Except to each other. In Iowa, court can waive ban.

(g) Three-month residency required before final judgment.

(h) Ground available to husband, also.

(i) No residency requirement before filing suit, but final decree cannot be entered until party is a resident for 6 months.

(j) Incurable.

(k) In some cases a lesser period of time may be allowed.

(l) Fraud, force, or duress.

(m) Mental incompetence.

(n) Parties related by marriage or blood, contrary to statute.

(o) Mental incapacity at time of marriage.

(p) In the discretion of the court.

(q) After expiration of term of separation decree.

(r) Loathsome disease.

(s) Attempt on life of spouse by poison or other means showing malice.

(t) No decree until parties have lived apart for 60 days.

(u) Must be domiciled in state and grounds occurred in state; 2 years separation need not have been in state.

(v) Spouse who obtained separation from bed and board may obtain absolute divorce 1 year after decree of separation becomes final. Other party may obtain decree 1 year and 60 days from the date of the separation decree.

(w) Attempt by either parent to corrupt son or prostitute daughter, or proposal by husband to prostitute wife.

(x) One year if cause occurred out of state and 2 years if on grounds of insanity.

(y) Voluntary living apart for 1 year and no reasonable expectation of reconciliation, or living separate and apart without cohabitation or interruption for 3 years.

DIVORCE LAWS AS OF DECEMBER 31, 1977* —Concluded

Grounds for absolute divorce

State or other jurisdiction	Non-support by husband	Insanity	Pregnancy at marriage	Big-amy	Un-explained absence	Felony conviction or imprison-ment	Other	Period before parties may remarry after final decree	
								Plaintiff	Defendant
Alabama	•	5 yrs.	•	...	...	•	(e)	60 days(f)	60 days(f)
Alaska	•	18 mos	...	...	...	•	...	...	...
Arizona	...	...	...	...	...	...	...	...	...
Arkansas	•(h)	3 yrs.	...	•	...	•	...	...	...
California	...	(j)	...	...	...	...	...	...	...
Colorado	...	...	...	...	...	...	...	...	...
Connecticut	...	5 yrs.	...	...	7 yrs.	•	(l)	...	...
Delaware	...	...	...	...	...	...	...	...	...
Florida	...	3 yrs.(m)	...	...	...	...	...	...	...
Georgia	...	2 yrs.	•	...	...	•	(l,n,o)	(p)	(p)
Hawaii	...	...	...	...	...	...	...	...	...
Idaho	•	3 yrs	...	...	...	•	...	...	...
Illinois	...	...	...	•	...	•	(r,s)	...	...
Indiana	...	2 yrs.	...	...	...	•	...	...	...
Iowa	...	...	...	...	...	...	...	1 yr.(f)	1 yr.(f)
Kansas	•	5 yrs.	...	...	...	•	...	30 days	30 days
Kentucky	...	...	...	...	...	...	...	...	...
Louisiana	...	...	...	...	...	...	...	...	...
Maine	•	...	...	...	...	...	...	...	...
Maryland	•	3 yrs.	...	...	...	•	(z)	...	...
Massachusetts	•	...	...	...	...	•	...	...	...
Michigan	...	...	...	...	...	...	...	...	...
Minnesota	...	...	...	...	...	...	...	6 mos.(f)	6 mos.(f)
Mississippi	...	3 yrs.	...	•	...	•	(n,aa)	...	(ab)
Missouri	...	...	...	...	...	...	...	...	...
Montana	...	...	...	...	...	...	...	...	...
Nebraska	...	...	...	...	...	...	...	...	...
Nevada	...	2 yrs.	...	...	...	...	...	...	...
New Hampshire	•	...	...	...	2 yrs.	•	(ac,ad)	...	...
New Jersey	...	2 yrs	...	...	...	•	(ae)	...	...
New Mexico	...	...	...	...	...	...	...	...	...
New York	(ag)	5 yrs.(af)	...	...	...	•	...	...	...
North Carolina	...	3 yrs.	•	...	...	•	(e)	...	...
North Dakota	•(h)	5 yrs.	...	...	...	•	...	(p)	(p)
Ohio	•(h)	4 yrs.	...	•	...	•	(l,ai)	...	...
Oklahoma	•(h)	5 yrs.	•	...	...	•	(l,ai)	6 mos.	6 mos.
Oregon	...	...	...	...	...	...	...	60 days	60 days
Pennsylvania	...	3 yrs.	...	•	...	•	(l,n,ak)	...	(al)
Rhode Island	•	...	...	...	•	...	(an,ao)	6 mos.	6 mos.
South Carolina	...	...	...	...	...	...	...	...	...
South Dakota	•	5 yrs.	...	...	...	•	...	...	...
Tennessee	•	...	...	•	...	•	(s,aq)	...	...
Texas	...	3 yrs.	...	...	...	•	...	30 days(f)	30 days(f)
Utah	•(h)	(ar)	...	...	...	•	...	...	...
Vermont	•(h)	5 yrs.	...	...	...	•	...	...	...
Virginia	...	...	...	...	...	•	...	...	...
Washington	...	...	...	...	...	...	...	...	...
West Virginia	...	3 yrs.	...	...	...	•	...	...	...
Wisconsin	•	1 yr.	...	...	...	•	...	6 mos.	6 mos.
Wyoming	•	2 yrs.	•	...	...	•	(av,aw)	...	...
Dist. of Col.	...	...	...	...	...	...	...	...	...
Puerto Rico	...	7 yrs.	...	...	10 yrs.	...	(w)	...	301 days

adopted the principle of *comparative rectitude*. In these states, a divorce is granted to the party who is "less at fault," with the judge being given wide discretion in making such a decision.

In some states there is a cutoff period or statute of limitations for adultery. In New York an action for divorce based on adultery must be brought within five years after discovery of the offense.

As noted previously, adultery is rarely used as a ground for divorce in noncontested cases. To avoid embarrassment, the parties usually prefer to base their case on some other provision of the law.

Cruelty is recognized as grounds for divorce in many states. Some of these states use explicit descriptions such as "extreme cruelty," "intolerable cruelty," or "cruel and inhuman treatment."

It is not always clear what constitutes cruelty. In some states there must be a showing that the guilty spouse engaged in physical brutality. One court stated that the charge implies a merciless and savage disposition leading to conduct amounting to actual personal violence.

What type of proof is required? In most states the person filing for divorce must show that the behavior took place over a period of time or that there was a pattern of misconduct. A court will usually not grant a divorce on the basis of one isolated example of violence. There are some exceptions, however. In one Pennsylvania case, a wife armed herself with a revolver and deliberately opened fire on her husband as he came up the stairs from the basement. She continued firing until the gun was empty, three of the six shots hitting the husband in the forehead, chest, and shoulder. The court concluded that the husband was entitled to a decree of divorce based on the wife's cruel and barbarous treatment.

In some states it is possible to get a divorce for "mental cruelty." This can be loosely defined as conduct which endangers mental well-being or makes it unsafe for the parties to continue living together. It can include threats of physical violence, cursing and obscene language, refusal to have sexual relations, and unjustified allegations of infidelity. In some places, even habitual nagging may be enough to constitute cruelty.

Sometimes a court may refuse to grant a divorce if it finds the defendant was provoked. In one case, a husband claimed that his wife threatened him with bodily harm, publicly insulted and ridiculed him, and accused him of adultery. The evidence showed, however, that this behavior was usually preceded by an act of the husband which demonstrated callous disregard for his wife. For example, the husband took a two-week trip to Florida with a young woman and went to Paris to visit another. The court held that under these circumstances, the wife's conduct, though unreasonable, was excusable because of the husband's provocation.

Under Pennsylvania law, a divorce can be granted for "cruel and barbarous treatment" and also for "indignities to the person." Indignities to the person may consist of vulgarity, habitual humiliating treatment, intentional incivility, or any other behavior which shows "that the love and affection upon which the matrimonial status rests has been permanently replaced by hatred and estrangement."

In one case, heard in 1954, a husband testified that his wife failed to keep house, neglected to care for the children, and often refused to prepare meals. The condition of the house was so bad that the board of health had to come in to clean it. The court placed most of the blame on the wife and decided that the husband was entitled to a divorce on the ground of "indignities."

Desertion, or *abandonment*, is often used as grounds for divorce in noncontested cases. To prove desertion, you have to show that your spouse voluntarily left or abandoned you without just cause and without your consent.

Suppose your spouse packs up and leaves on a Saturday afternoon. Can you file for a divorce on Monday? The answer is no. There is a minimum period of time which must elapse before you can prove desertion. This period of time is set by state law. In New York it is one year; in Pennsylvania it is two years. You must be able to show that the desertion was continuous for the entire period. If you and your spouse agree to resume living together, even for one day, the time period is cut off and you have to start all over again.

Under the law the separation has to be voluntary and without justification. If one spouse is inducted into military service or is committed to a mental institution, for example, it is not considered desertion or abandonment.

Sometimes you can get a divorce if you are able to show that you have been forced to leave the house or have been locked out. In some states this is known as "constructive desertion." The theory is that the spouse remaining in the house has actually deserted the other by forcing him or her to find a new place to live. In one case, a husband testified that his wife attacked him with a bread knife, called him a bum, and threatened to kill him if he did not leave. The court ruled that the wife had excluded him from the common domicile in such a way as to constitute a willful and malicious desertion on her part.

Insanity is frequently recognized as a ground for divorce. Although the exact requirements differ in each jurisdiction, you can generally assume that neurotic or mildly abnormal behavior is not enough to establish insanity. In most states, your spouse has to be declared legally insane or has to be confined to a mental institution for a prescribed period of time.

Impotency is also recognized as a ground for divorce in many states. Under the law, there are usually two elements which must be established: first, that the spouse was impotent at the time of the marriage, and second, that the impotency is incurable.

Suppose that your spouse is *confined in prison*. Can you get a divorce? In most states you can, although in some the imprisonment must be for a serious crime such as murder, assault, arson, or robbery. Some statutes provide that the guilty spouse must be confined in prison for a specified number of years. (In New York, the time period is three years.)

Drunkenness is listed as a separate ground for divorce in some states. This does not mean that you can establish a case on the basis of one or two incidents. To prove drunkenness, you usually have to show that your spouse cannot—or will not—keep away from the bottle. In some states, you can also obtain a divorce if your spouse has a serious drug habit.

No-Fault Divorce

Some states still operate under the antiquated "fault" theory of divorce. The person filing for a divorce must allege that he or she is innocent and that the other person is totally at fault. Of course, marital breakups are usually not that clear-cut. What usually happens is that both parties contribute to the problem. Or the marriage simply disintegrates—the husband and wife find that they have different interests or career goals, or that they no longer enjoy spending time together. In these situations, it is illogical and unfair to require that all the blame be placed on one person.

Some states have remedied this problem by adopting "no-fault" divorce. In these jurisdictions, a divorce can be granted without fixing blame on one of the parties. In California, for example, a husband and wife can get a divorce for *irreconcilable differences which have caused the irremediable breakdown of the marriage*. In simple terms, this means that the husband and wife can't get along and that there is very little likelihood that they will be able to patch things up.

In some states, such as Florida and Alabama, a no-fault divorce can be obtained if there is an *irretrievable breakdown* of the marriage. (For a complete list of no-fault states, see the chart on pages 78–79.)

Residence Requirements

Suppose a married couple lives in a state which still operates under the old "fault" concept. They decide that they want to get a divorce, but neither one wants to file papers charging the other with some offense such as cruelty, desertion, or drunkenness. Why can't they simply hop on a plane, fly to California, and get a divorce for "irreconcilable differences"? The answer is that California, like most states, has a *residence requirement* which must be met before a divorce will be granted. Under California law, one of the parties must be a resident of the state for six months and a resident of the county in which the proceeding is filed for three months.

Forty-eight states impose such a residency requirement as a condition for obtaining a divorce. As might be expected, the time periods vary from state to state, ranging from six weeks to two years. The most common requirement is one year.

How do you establish that you are a resident of a particular state? You must usually show that you have been physically present within the state and that you have a real intention to make it your fixed and permanent home. Your intention must be bona fide and not merely for the purpose of obtaining a divorce. If you leave the state to take a vacation or to sign up for a four-week French course at the Sorbonne in Paris, it will probably not affect your legal status, as long as you leave with the intention of returning to your permanent home.

Residency requirements can sometimes be a serious impediment. In one recent case a woman moved to Iowa with her two children and, after one month, filed a petition for divorce. The court dismissed the petition because the woman did not meet the statutory requirement of one year's residency in that state. The woman filed suit in federal court, claiming that the residency law was unconstitutional because it discriminated against people who had recently moved to the state by denying them access to the only method they had of legally dissolving their marriage. The Supreme Court ruled that the residency requirement was constitutional and observed that a "state such as Iowa may quite reasonably decide that it does not wish to become a divorce mill for unhappy spouses who have lived there as short a time as [the woman] had when she commenced her action in the state court . . ."

You may have heard that it is possible to obtain a "quickie" divorce in Haiti, the Dominican Republic, or some other foreign country. While it is true that in come countries it is possible to obtain a divorce (with the consent of your spouse) in a matter of days, there are some drawbacks that you should know about. First, you will have to retain a lawyer in this country to prepare some forms and make the necessary arrangements, and second, the total bill, including air fare, hotel accommodations, and legal fees, will probably be much higher than that for an American divorce.

Do-It-Yourself Divorce Kits

Now that the divorce laws have been simplified in many states, more and more people are filing papers *pro se*, or on their own behalf. A court clerk in Portland, Oregon, has estimated that about ten people a week represent themselves in divorce proceedings there. And according to a report in a national magazine, about 25% of the divorces in Southern California are obtained without legal representation.

It is not possible in this chapter to provide detailed step-by-step instructions, because each state has its own separate divorce procedures. However, in many states you can find out all that you need to know by buying a "do-it-yourself" divorce kit. The kits are available in bookstores and through newspaper ads. The kits usually contain information about divorce procedures in your state, sample forms, and instructions on how to file papers in court.

When these kits first appeared, they were opposed by some members of the legal profession and by some bar associations. Attempts were even made in a few cases to block the publication and sale of these kits on the ground that they constituted "the unauthorized practice of law." In most instances, these attempts were not successful. In the early 1970s, the State of New York filed suit against one individual to stop him from selling "The Divorce Yourself Kit" to the public. The state won in the lower court, but the decision was reversed on appeal. The court noted that "the defendant's publication does not purport to give personal advice on a specific problem peculiar to a designated or readily identified person, and because of the absence of the essential element of 'legal practice—the representation and the advising of a particular person in a particular situation'—in the publication and sale of the kits, such publication and sale did not constitute the unlawful practice of law." However, the court ruled that the defendant could not give advice to individual people about their specific divorce problems.

If you are planning to buy a do-it-yourself divorce kit, check to see that the following subjects are covered:

1. *Grounds for divorce.* The kit should give you information about the specific grounds for divorce in your state. (There should also be sample forms which can be used in most cases.)

2. *Proof.* The kit should tell you what type of proof is needed to obtain a divorce. If your case is based on cruelty, for example, you may have to bring witnesses to court to testify that they were present when your spouse slapped you or threatened to injure you.

3. *Residence.* The kit should provide an explanation of the residence requirements in your state.

4. *Serving the papers.* The kit should explain how to serve the divorce petition on your spouse and how to file the petition in court.

5. *Filing fees.* The kit should tell you how much money you will have to pay for court costs and filing fees. (The total cost usually amounts to less than $100.)

6. *Alimony.* The kit should explain how to provide for alimony payments and the division of all of the property and assets owned by you and your spouse.

7. *Custody of children.* The kit should tell you how to arrange for custody of your children (assuming that there is no dispute on this point) and how to arrange for visitation rights for the other spouse.

8. *Child support.* The kit should also tell you how to provide for child-support payments in the decree.

If you have any questions about your case, you can usually obtain information from one of the clerks in court. These clerks are not permitted to serve as legal counsel, but they are familiar with the divorce laws and with all of the forms which must be completed.

If many states, you have to appear in court and give testimony before a divorce will be granted. Naturally, this may make you a little nervous, but if all of your papers are in order, the entire procedure may take less than ten minutes.

Annulments

The practical effects of an annulment and a divorce are similar, but legally, the two are quite different. When a divorce is granted, the court rules that the marriage is terminated. When an annulment is granted, however, the court declares that a valid marriage never existed.

The grounds for an annulment vary from state to state, but the most common ones are:

1. Bigamy.
2. Marriage before attaining legal age.
3. Impotency or physical incapacity.
4. Fraud.
5. Mental illness or insanity.

In one case, a woman claimed that her husband suffered from a mental disorder known as voyeurism which caused him to peek into house windows and to engage in acts of indecent exposure. There was evidence that the mental disorder existed prior to the marriage and that the husband did not tell his wife anything about his condition until they had been married for six years. The court granted the wife's application for an annulment and stated that the husband had an affirmative duty to disclose this condition to his wife before marriage.

In New York, annulments are often granted on the basis of fraud. A wife may claim, for example, that before marriage her husband falsely represented that he intended to have children. The judge will usually annul the marriage on these grounds when no opposition is raised by the husband.

The allegations made in annulment petitions are sometimes bizarre. In one petition, one woman claimed that before she was married, her husband concealed from her the fact that he had been an officer in the German army and a member of the Nazi party during World War II, that he was fanatically anti-Semitic, and that he advocated and even applauded Hitler's "final solution" of the Jewish question, namely the extermination of the Jewish people. The woman claimed that after they were married, her husband demanded that she "weed out" all of her Jewish friends and stop socializing with them. The husband tried to have the case dismissed, but the Court of Appeals, the highest court in New York State, ruled that the wife was entitled to a hearing. The court observed that a "fanatical conviction . . . that a race or group of people living in the same community should be put to death as at Auschwitz, Belsen, Dachau, or Buchenwald" is evidence of a diseased mind. "The continuation of [the husband's] addiction to this anti-social and fanatical objective after and during marriage, which had been concealed and inferentially misrepresented during courtship, would so plainly make the marital relationship unworkable in this jurisdiction . . . that it would depart from the realities to conclude that it was not essential to this married relationship or that [the wife] would have consented to the marriage without its concealment."

Legal Separations

Some marriage relationships seem to drift about in limbo. The husband and wife may live separate and apart for months, or even years, without taking any specific action. Then one of them grows unhappy with the arrangement for some reason and files for a *legal separation*.

The laws concerning legal separation vary from state to state. In some states, a husband and wife can obtain a "judicial separation" or, as it is sometimes called, "a separation from bed and board." Usually, the person who files for a separation must allege grounds. (The grounds for a separation are not always the same as for divorce, although in some cases they do overlap.)

Why would someone file for a legal separation rather than a divorce? Usually it is because there are no grounds for divorce or because the other spouse has threatened to contest the divorce proceedings. In some cases, a wife may file for a legal separation in order to obtain support payments from her husband. Or the wife may use the separation action as a tactical ploy; once the husband realizes that he will have to make support payments anyway, he may drop his objections and consent to the divorce.

In some cases, both the husband and the wife are reluctant to end the marriage. For these couples, a legal separation is seen as a halfway measure which leaves the door open for a reconciliation.

A husband and wife can usually file an application in court to revoke a separation decree. In New York, both the husband and the wife have to join in the application. The court may grant the application without qualification or it may impose any regulations or restrictions that it deems reasonable.

In some states a judicial separation can be used as the basis for a divorce action. Before divorce papers are filed, the parties must live apart for a certain period of time pursuant to the terms of the separation decree.

Sometimes a husband and wife who are having marital difficulties decide to sign a *written separation agreement*. They agree to live separate and apart, and each promises not to molest, bother, or interfere with the other. Arrangements are usually made in the agreement for the division of all property and bank accounts. If the couple has children, there are usually provisions made for custody and visitation rights. In most cases, the husband will agree to make periodic payments for alimony and child support. For legal and financial reasons it is usually best to specify how much is allocated for alimony and how much for child support. In some agreements, there are provisions which require the husband to pay for medical bills or for college tuition for the children.

From a legal standpoint, the separation agreement is treated like a contract. Once you sign the agreement, you are stuck with it—unless you can convince your spouse to amend or modify the provisions.

In New York, a written separation agreement can be used as

the basis for a divorce action. But first the husband and wife have to live separate and apart for one year pursuant to the agreement.

Alimony

For many couples the most important issue in a divorce proceeding is alimony. Since the financial circumstances of each case are different, the court is granted wide latitude in determining whether a wife should receive alimony, and if so, how much. The court will usually consider a number of factors, including the length of the marriage, the ability of the wife to be self-supporting, and the financial resources and standard of living of the parties.

Can a court award alimony to the husband? Yes. Recently, the Supreme Court ruled that a state law that provides that only wives may receive alimony is unconstitutional. The court stated that "the old notion that generally it is the man's primary responsibility to provide a home and its essentials can no longer justify a statute that discriminates on the basis of gender."

This decision has not caused a major turnabout in support patterns; it is still extremely rare for a husband to receive alimony payments from his wife. Some changes, though, have taken place. Alimony has become more and more a means of assisting a needy spouse, with the amount of alimony based on the actual need of one spouse and the ability of the other to pay. If the wife is self-supporting, she usually agrees to forgo alimony payments entirely, unless, of course, the wife earns much less than her husband. If the wife earns $15,000 a year, and the husband $80,000, some provision will usually be made for alimony.

In noncontested cases it is customary for the husband and wife to work out a financial arrangement in advance—before any papers are filed in court. In most cases, the court will accept a *stipulation* or agreement between the husband and wife on the amount of alimony to be paid.

In some states, which still operate under the old "fault" concept, the wife cannot get alimony if she is the "guilty" party. This rule has been changed in some places, but—all things being equal—it still pays for the wife to file for the divorce, rather than the husband, to ensure that she will receive alimony.

Many divorce decrees provide that the husband must make

alimony payments on a monthly basis. Understandably, the husband may not be overjoyed at the prospect of sending checks to his ex-wife every month. Instead, he may try to settle all his obligations at once by asking the court to award the wife one large, *lump-sum* payment. The husband can sometimes benefit from this type of arrangement, but there are some negative factors which must be considered. For one thing, the lump-sum payment may not be tax-deductible; see the discussion of this point later in this chapter. For another thing, the husband cannot be certain that, with the lump-sum payment, he is totally off the hook. If his ex-wife runs through all the money she receives and has no other means of support, she may be able to go back to court and get more money from him.

Suppose the husband and wife decide that alimony payments should be made on a monthly basis. How long does the husband have to keep making such payments? As a general rule, alimony payments must continue until the husband or wife dies or the wife remarries. Some states, however, have special provisions. For example, New Hampshire limits alimony to three years and then provides for renewal if the recipient has been unable to join the labor force. If the husband is elderly or in poor health, the wife may insist on a lump-sum payment to avoid any possible problems. Or she may try to get her husband to agree—as part of the divorce settlement—that alimony payments will continue even after his death. Then if the husband dies, the alimony payments will be made by his estate—as long as he leaves sufficient assets.

Sometimes the wife has to take into account other factors, such as the husband's future earning capacity. Suppose the husband is a resident in a hospital making $15,000 a year. In a few years he may have his own medical practice and be earning four or five times that amount. Naturally, this point should be raised by the wife in any discussions about alimony.

The amount of alimony fixed in a decree may be raised or lowered if there is *a substantial change in circumstances*. If the wife loses her job, for example, and has to accept part-time work at $100 a week, she can usually go to court and ask for an "upward modification" of the alimony payments. On the other hand, if the husband is laid off or unable to work, he can ask the court to reduce the amount of the payments. In any case, the court will act only when there is a *substantial* change in circumstances. If the husband loses a week's pay because of illness, for example, the court will not lower the amount of his alimony payments.

What if an ex-wife establishes a close relationship with another man and moves into his apartment? Can her alimony payments be cut off?

In New York, alimony payments can be terminated only if the ex-wife "is habitually living with another man *and* holding herself out as his wife." In one case a wife was granted a divorce from her husband and awarded alimony in the amount of $160 a month. Several months later, the husband went back to court and asked that the alimony payments be terminated. He presented proof that his ex-wife was living with another man, shared the same bedroom with him, cooked meals, did his wash, and shared household expenses with him. But there was no evidence that she had ever "held herself out" as being married to this man. As a result, the court ruled that the husband had to continue to make alimony payments.

There has been some pressure on the New York legislature to change this law. Other states have already adopted a different policy. In one case in Minnesota, a husband signed an agreement in 1972 promising to pay his wife alimony "until such time as she remarries or dies." Four years later, he discovered that his former wife was having a sexual relationship with another woman. The court ruled that this relationship was cause for terminating the husband's obligation to pay alimony: "Defendant has discovered that her sexual orientation is lesbian. . . . At the time of the 1972 divorce, plaintiff could have realistically assumed that the defendant would remarry. . . . Plaintiff would not have entered into a stipulation to pay alimony until defendant remarried or died, had he realized that remarriage was or would become impossible. Defendant's post-decree lesbianism is a material change in circumstances, which justifies the termination of alimony."

Some states have enacted laws to protect husbands in such situations. In Connecticut, for example, the courts can end alimony payments when economic need is removed—whether the former wife is living with a man, a woman, or her parents.

Child Custody

Before you file for a divorce, you should try to come to an agreement with your spouse about who will have custody of the children. The court will usually abide by your decision unless there is some reason to believe that the person who is designated will not be able to care for the children properly.

If there is a dispute about child custody, the court will have to resolve the issue. A number of factors must be weighed by the court, but the overriding consideration is *the best interests of the child*. In recent years, many husbands have been able to win custody of their children by showing that they can provide the necessary love and affection. But it still seems that in close cases, the wife usually has the edge—especially if the children are young.

If you are involved in a custody dispute, don't try to handle it yourself. Find a competent lawyer—one who has experience in divorce proceedings—and let him argue your case in court.

In some custody disputes, the children themselves express a preference for one parent over the other. This can be a factor in the court's decision, although it is by no means the only one. Usually it carries more weight if the children are older and capable of exercising sound judgment.

A ruling granting custody to one of the parties is not necessarily written in stone. It can be altered or modified at a later time, but only if there has been a change of circumstances or if the parent who has custody neglects to care for the children.

When custody is awarded to one of the parents, the court will usually provide the other with "reasonable visitation rights." In most cases, the court will accept a stipulation or agreement by the parties setting forth the specific times for visitation. If the wife is awarded custody, the husband should try to get the right to see the children once or twice a week. The husband should also bargain for visitation on major holidays and for one or two weeks each summer when the children are on vacation.

Child Support

If the wife obtains custody of the children, the husband still has an obligation to help support them. This is true even if the wife has a high-paying job or has a substantial amount of money in the bank. The divorce decree will usually specify how much the husband has to pay for support. On this point the court will consider a number of factors, including the financial resources of the parties, the husband's income, and the needs of the children. As a rule, support payments must continue until the children marry or reach the age of majority (usually eighteen to twenty-one depending on state law). But the husband can agree in a written stipulation or separation agreement to have the payments continue until the children are older.

Before you file for a divorce, you should speak to your spouse and try to settle on a fair amount for child-support payments. The judge will usually accept any figure you come up with unless it appears to be too low to meet the needs of your children. Like alimony, child-support payments can be raised or lowered at a later time if there is a substantial change of circumstances.

There is no precise formula for determining the amount of payments. In most cases, the husband pays between 20% and 40% of his income for child-support payments and alimony payments combined. If the husband has a substantial income, the percentage sometimes turns out to be less.

In addition to child-support payments, the husband may have to assume certain other financial responsibilities. The wife may insist, as part of the divorce settlement, that the husband take out hospitalization insurance on the children, or she may ask him to pay for "extraordinary medical and dental expenses," such as allergy treatments or orthodontic work. In some cases, the husband is also asked to pay for all, or part, of the children's college tuition or postgraduate training.

Other Factors

Before you go to court, you should decide what to do with all of the property and other assets you have acquired. If you own a house, you have two basic options: You can sell the house and divide the proceeds, or you can keep it and arrange for one person to remain in possession after the divorce. If you have children, you may decide that it is best to give the house to the one who will be awarded custody of the children under the final decree. Before you make any plans, though, you should check the deed to see who has "title" to the property. In most cases, the deed will specify that the property is owned jointly by you and your spouse. If one of you is going to remain in the house after the divorce, it may be necessary to prepare a new deed to reflect a change in ownership. In such a situation, you should hire an attorney to make certain that the property is transferred in accordance with state law.

If you live in an apartment rather than a house, there are still some arrangements that you will have to make. First, you will have to decide who is going to remain in the apartment after the divorce action is started. Then you will have to take a look at the lease agreement. In most cases, you will find that both you and your spouse have signed the document—which means that both of you are liable to the landlord for rent payments. If your name is on the lease and you are planning to move out, you can ask your spouse to sign a letter of agreement promising to "indemnify" you for any rent payments that you will have to make to the landlord. To be safe, though, you should ask your landlord to draw up a new lease—one which will be signed only by your spouse.

Next, you have to decide what to do with all of your other property, including money in savings accounts, investment holdings, stocks and bonds, automobiles, and household furniture.* Usually, the court will accept any arrangement that you make for the division of property.

Obviously, the arrangements made for dividing the property will have an effect on the amount of alimony awarded. If the wife receives the house, the car, and most of the money in the bank, she will usually have to accept less in the way of alimony payments.

Before you make any decisions about alimony or child support, you should consider the tax consequences. Alimony payments to a former spouse are tax-deductible—if they are periodic in nature and made pursuant to the terms of a divorce decree, a separation decree, or a written separation agreement. Lump-sum payments are *not* deductible unless they are paid in installments over a period of more than ten years. But if you fall behind in making your regular payments and have to settle the amount in one lump sum, the total amount paid is then deductible.

Child-support payments are *not* deductible. This is one reason

---

* In those states which have community-property laws, all of the property acquired during the marriage by either spouse is, in effect, owned by both of them. States with community-property laws are Arizona, California, Idaho, Louisiana, Nevada, New Mexico, Texas, and Washington.

why it is important to specify clearly in the divorce decree or separation agreement exactly how much money is allocated for child support and how much for alimony.

The spouse who receives alimony payments must list the payments as income, but this is not the case with child-support payments. These factors can play an important part in the negotiations between the husband and wife. Consider this example:

Mr. and Mrs. Dunbar decide to get a divorce. Arrangements are made for Mrs. Dunbar to have custody of the two children, aged five and three, and to receive $300 each month for alimony and child support. The Dunbars reach an impasse, however, when it comes time to decide how to allocate the payments. Mr. Dunbar wants to specify that $200 of the total amount will go for alimony, so that he can deduct these payments from his gross income. But Mrs. Dunbar wants to have the $200 go for child support—and only $100 for alimony—so that she will have to pay less in taxes. In addition, she knows that if she remarries, she will lose the alimony payments, and therefore is in a better position if most of the money is paid for child support.

Suppose, though, that the children are older, say seventeen and fifteen. Then Mrs. Dunbar will probably want to have most of the money listed as alimony, since she will lose the support payments when the children reach the age of majority.

If you are making arrangements for alimony and child support, you should also discuss *exemptions*. Under the provisions of the tax code, you are allowed a $1,000 exemption for every person who qualifies as a "dependent." You should try to include a provision in the divorce decree or separation agreement specifying who will get to take the children as exemptions. It is possible to give the exemptions to the parent without custody if he or she pays at least $600 per year for the support of each child. If no provision is made in the divorce decree or separation agreement for these exemptions, the parent without custody can still claim exemptions if he or she pays at least $1,200 per year for the support of each child *and* contributes more than the parent who has custody. For more information about taxes, write to the IRS and ask for a publication entitled "Tax Information for Divorced or Separated Individuals."

Some couples have no trouble dealing with important financial matters, but they argue over minor issues such as who gets to keep the paperback books or the household plants. No specific advice can be offered on how to divide personal property, but it is suggested that you try to keep a sense of proportion during your discussions.

Several years ago, a couple in Hutchinson, Kansas, became entangled in a dispute over who should have permanent custody of the family cat. A year after their divorce, they took the matter to court. The judge gave custody of the cat to the wife, but he ruled that the former husband was entitled to visitation rights.

Palimony

In the last few years there has been a substantial increase in the number of couples living together without marrying. These couples usually try to avoid legal and financial disputes by keeping their relationships informal. But what happens when they split up? Is any provision made for the division of property? If one person has earned a substantial amount of money, should the other receive support payments—or *palimony*—as compensation for the time and energy expended during the relationship?

These issues have gained wide attention in the wake of the Lee Marvin case. Marvin, a Hollywood actor who is best known for his portrayal of tough guys and gunfighters, decided to live with Michelle Triola in October 1964. When the couple split up seven years later, Michelle filed suit, asking for a distribution of property and for support payments. She claimed that in 1964 she and Marvin had entered into an oral agreement that "while the parties lived together they would combine their efforts and earnings and would share equally any and all property accumulated as a result of their efforts." She said that shortly thereafter she agreed to "give up her lucrative career as an entertainer and singer" in order to devote herself full-time to Marvin as a companion, homemaker, housekeeper, and cook; in return he agreed to provide for all of her financial needs and support for the rest of her life.

Marvin tried to have the complaint dismissed on legal grounds, but the Supreme Court of California ruled that Michelle had a right to take the case to trial. The court held that oral agreements between unmarried partners to divide property or provide support are enforceable: "The fact that a man and woman live together without marriage, and engage in a sexual relationship, does not in itself invalidate agreements between them relating to their earnings, property or expenses."

Then the court went one step further. It held that even if there was no express agreement, the court could find that there was an "implied agreement" based on the couple's conduct: ". . . In the absence of an express agreement, the courts may look to a variety of other remedies in order to protect the parties' lawful expectations.

"The courts may inquire into the conduct of the parties to determine whether that conduct demonstrates an implied contract or implied agreement."

When the Marvin case finally went to trial, the judge decided that there was, in fact, no express or implied agreement between the parties, but he did award Michelle Triola $104,000 for purposes of "rehabilitation."

It is still too early to know what the effects of the Marvin case will be. In California it is still possible to collect from your former roommate if you can prove that you had an express or implied agreement to share income. In other states, like New York, which take a more conservative approach, it is unlikely that you will be able to recover money by claiming that you had an oral agreement.

Is there anything you can do—in advance—to avoid these legal tangles? The only surefire protection is to enter into a specific *written agreement* stating exactly how all of your assets and property will be divided in the event that you split up. This is ironic, because many couples opt for a live-in relationship, rather than a marriage, because they want to avoid making any formal commitments.

If you are living with someone, the Marvin case will probably have very little impact on your relationship. If you break up, you will have to decide how to divide all of the things that you purchased together. But "palimony" will probably not be a factor unless you or your live-in companion has a bundle of money.

7

Credit Problems

One of the most serious problems you can have is a bad credit rating. If you are a typical consumer, you probably purchase most of your household appliances, furniture, and even clothing by using credit. According to government figures, the amount of consumer credit outstanding has grown from $125 billion in 1970 to over $300 billion in 1978. Reports also indicate that there are now well over 500 million credit cards in use by consumers. Most people, however, use these credit cards without ever understanding what legal rights they have in the event there is a dispute with the company extending the credit.

Credit Cards

A credit card is a plastic or metal card, with your name and account number embossed on it, which you present when you wish to purchase products or services on credit. The principal advantage of carrying credit cards is their convenience; you can purchase almost any item you need without having to carry around large sums of money.

For general purposes, there are three types of credit cards. The first type is issued by such companies as retail stores, airlines, and gasoline companies and can be used to buy goods or services only from the company that issues the card. For example, if you have a credit card from Bloomingdale's Department Store, you can use the card to make purchases at Bloomingdale's but not from an airline or at a gas station. The second type of credit card is issued by banks. These cards—such as Master Card and Visa—

are widely honored by all kinds of businesses, both nationally and internationally, including retail stores, restaurants, hotels, and car-rental companies. The third type of card is issued by national credit-card companies, such as American Express, Diner's Club, and Carte Blanche. These companies charge their card users an annual membership fee.

Credit-card applications are distributed in many places, such as banks, department stores, and other retail outlets. Companies that issue credit cards will usually approve your application only after they have checked your credit rating and determined that you are a good risk. Some, for example, will issue a card only if you make $10,000 a year or more and have a solid employment record.

In nearly every case, the credit-card company will limit the amount of credit you can obtain. If you make $10,000 for example, a major bank credit-card company may limit your credit to $500 when you are first accepted. But if you make regular payments and demonstrate that you are a good credit risk, the company may raise the limit to $1,000 or more.

In the past some companies sent out credit cards to persons who had not either applied for them or authorized them. This was usually done for those persons who had a good credit record. Now, however, federal law prohibits sending a card without authorization, although a company is permitted to send a new card to persons whose current card expires.

If your credit card is lost or stolen, notify the company *immediately*. Check your records to see if the company has issued instructions or supplied a form for use in reporting the loss of your card. If you notify the company immediately, you will not be responsible for more than $50 in charges—and you won't have to pay even that amount if the charges were made after you notified the company. To avoid problems, notify the company by telephone at once, and then send in the company's forms or a follow-up letter like the one below:

March 1, 1980

Mr. Robert Smith
ABC Department Store
100 Broad Street
Chicago, Illinois

Dear Mr. Smith:
Confirming our telephone conversation today, I want to report that my credit card was stolen this afternoon while I was shopping.

This letter will confirm that I am not responsible for any charges made with my card. The number of the card is 673 014 230 and is listed under my full name, Cathryn T. Consumer.

Thank you.

Very truly yours,
Cathryn Consumer

Sometimes you can save money by *not* using a credit card. Occasionally a merchant will offer a discount of up to 5% to customers who pay by cash or check. You are entitled to take advantage of such an offer even if you have a credit-card account. While a merchant can offer a discount to cash-paying customers, he is not allowed to charge you more than the list price if you do decide to use your credit card.

Credit Payments

One of the principal advantages of using a credit card is that you can buy now and pay later. The standard practice is for the credit-card company to send a monthly bill or statement containing a list of your purchases. The company is required by law to specify on the bill a date by which your payment must be received by the company.

All credit-card companies have a monthly *billing cycle*. The billing cycle is the length of time from one billing statement to the next. Under the law, the credit-card company must mail the statement to you at least fourteen days before the end of the billing cycle. For example, if you have a credit-card account with a monthly cycle that ends on the 20th of the month, the company must mail your statement by the 6th of the month at the latest. This will give you at least two weeks in which to make your payment so that it is reflected as a credit to your account on the following statement.

Most credit-card companies, such as Master Card, offer the option of extending your payments over a period of several months if you do not want to pay your bill in full immediately. If you decide to extend your payments, you will have to pay a finance charge, which is computed on the unpaid balance. In most cases, the finance charge is 18% a year (or 1½% a month) for the first $500 of the outstanding balance, and 12% a year (or 1% a month) for the amount over $500. Companies usually require a minimum monthly payment based on the total amount due.

Consumers sometimes purchase automobiles and other major items on credit by signing a *retail installment contract*. (See Chapter 2, on contracts.) Under the terms of these contracts, the consumer makes an initial down payment and agrees to pay the balance of the purchase price in installments. As a general rule the contract will give the dates when payments are due, the amount of each payment, and the amount of the finance charge. In the case of automobiles and other expensive items, the finance charge can amount to several hundred dollars.

If the buyer fails to make payments on time, the contract may provide for delinquency or penalty charges. The contract may also have an acceleration clause which states that if the buyer fails to pay an installment, the seller can demand full payment immediately.

Billing Disputes

Suppose you buy a television set from a department store with your credit card, but when you receive your monthly bill from the store, you find that you have been charged too much. What can you do?

The Fair Credit Billing Act now protects you against unfair and inaccurate billing practices. The law requires the store to follow certain procedures whenever a customer complains that there has been a "billing error." A billing error can take place when:

1. You are charged for something that you didn't buy.
2. You are charged too much for something that you did buy.
3. Your bill lists a charge and you can't figure out what it refers to or what it means.
4. The goods or services were not delivered to you according to your agreement with the store. For example, the store failed to deliver the right merchandise.
5. You made a payment or returned goods and your account was not properly credited.
6. A mistake in arithmetic was made in figuring your bill, or the store added a finance charge or a late-payment charge without just cause.

If you have a billing problem like one of those mentioned above, you can ask the store to correct your account. You have 60 days from the date you receive the billing statement to write to the store about the mistake. (A telephone call will not protect your rights under this law.) Your letter should contain the following information:

1. Your name and charge-account number.
2. A statement that the company has made a billing error and the dollar amount of the error.
3. An explanation of why you think the billing statement contains an error.

Make a copy of the letter for your records. If your billing dispute involves a large sum of money, send the letter by certified mail, return receipt requested, so you will have proof that the letter was delivered.

The store must let you know within 30 days that it has received your letter, and it must give you its decision concerning the possible billing error within 90 days. Under the law, the store is required to either correct your statement or, after conducting an investigation, send you a written notice explaining why it believes there was no billing error. In either case, you can ask the company to send you sales receipts or other documentary evidence of the purchase.

While this procedure is going on, you are *not* required to pay the amount of money in dispute. Until the store gives you the reasons why it believes the charge is proper, it cannot force you to pay the charge—and it cannot require you to pay finance charges for the amount of money in dispute. The store may, however, use the disputed charge in deciding if you have reached your credit limit. Suppose, for example, that you are allowed to charge up to $500 on your account and you have already charged $400 worth of goods. If you get a bill for $500 (which includes a $100 charge for a vacuum cleaner that you never bought), the store can still say that you have reached your credit limit of $500 and that you cannot charge anything more on your account until you reduce the outstanding balance.

During this period the store cannot close your account or threaten to ruin your credit rating because you refuse to pay for the item. Remember, though, that while the billing dispute continues, you are responsible for paying amounts on the bill which are not in dispute.

What happens if the store determines that there has not been a billing error? Under the law, you have at least 10 days to pay the amount requested before the store can report your account as "delinquent." If your credit-card agreement provides for a longer period of time to pay regular bills, then the store cannot report you as delinquent until this longer period of time has passed.

If a store fails to respond to your letter, or violates any of your other rights, it forfeits the amount of money in dispute (together with any finance charges computed on that amount) up to a maximum of $50. This penalty is probably too light to serve as an effective deterrent, but remember that the penalty is assessed for any violation of the law, even if it turns out that no billing error was ever made.

If you write to a store about a billing error and the store's explanation does not satisfy you, you should write another letter to the store and say that you still believe there is a mistake. When this happens, the store is still allowed to try to collect the amount in dispute, but you gain several important advantages:

1. The store cannot notify a credit bureau that you are delinquent in your bill payment unless it also tells the credit bureau that you dispute the bill.
2. The store must send you the name and address of everyone who receives a report of your delinquency.
3. If the store later clears up your dispute, it must notify everyone who received the initial report that the dispute has been settled.

Again, if the store fails to follow these rules, it forfeits the amount of money in dispute (as well as finance charges) up to $50.

If you believe that the store has not followed these requirements, you can file suit under the Fair Credit Billing Act. If you win your suit in court, you can recover:

1. Damages for any actual financial injury which you sustained as a result of the violation.
2. Twice the amount of any finance charge involved.
3. Court costs and reasonable attorney's fees.

What happens if you make a mistake and pay too much money to the store? You can ask the store to refund the extra amount, provided it is more than $1. The store is obligated to refund the extra payment no later than 5 business days after it receives your letter. If you do not ask for a refund of the extra payment, the store has a choice: It can either credit your account or send you a refund.

Disputes Regarding Defective Merchandise

If you purchase goods from a store by using a national credit card, such as Master Card or Visa, and the goods turn out to be defective, are you obligated to pay the credit card company? Under the law, you can withhold payment if the goods are defective *and* you meet the following conditions:

1. The purchase price was more than $50.
2. The purchase was made in your state or within 100 miles of your mailing address.
3. You have made an honest effort to clear up the problem with the store that sold you the goods.

The credit-card company may not accept your claim that the goods are defective, but if they sue you to collect the amount in dispute, you can defend the suit by using any of the legal defenses that you could have used against the store that sold you the goods.

Suppose, for example, that you purchase a $400 television set from ABC Electronics and you use your Master Card to pay for it. When you get home you discover that the picture tube is on the blink. You take the set back to the store immediately, but the service manager refuses to repair the picture tube. Under these circumstances, you can withhold payment for the set. To protect your rights, however, you should send a letter to the credit-card company stating that the television set was defective and that the store refused to do anything about it. Most likely, the credit-card company will try to resolve the dispute. If the credit-card company takes you to court, you will probably win the suit—if you can show that the television set was defective.

What happens if you pay part of the money due to the credit-card company before you discover that the television set is defective? Your rights in that case are more limited. You can withhold only the unpaid amount of the item (together with any interest you have been charged on that amount). For example, if you had already paid $100 to the credit-card company, you would be entitled to withhold only the remaining $300.

There may be times when you purchase defective goods for $50 or less or when the purchase does not take place in the same state as your mailing address (or within 100 miles of that address).

In these cases, you can withhold payment if the company that sold you the goods

1. issued the credit card you used to make the purchase, or
2. is controlled by the company that issued the credit card, or
3. is a franchised dealer of the credit-card company, or
4. obtained your order through a mail solicitation made by the credit-card company.

If you have a dispute with a national credit-card company over defective merchandise, you can send a letter like the one below:

March 1, 1980

National Credit Card Company
Accounts Division
Box 100
New York, N. Y.

Re: Account No. 015 074 1644

Dear Sir:

On February 20, 1980, I purchased a new television set from ABC Electronics for $400. When I returned home, the picture tube was not working. I returned the set to ABC Electronics immediately, but the service manager refused to repair the picture tube or give me a credit for the purchase.

I have asked Standard Repair Service of 980 E. 23rd Street to examine the set and give me an estimate for repairs. I have been informed that my picture tube is defective and it will cost approximately $200 for a new tube.

Under the circumstances, I wish to cancel the sale and I request that you credit my account for the $400 price.

Very truly yours,
Cathryn Consumer

There may be special factors to consider if you use a credit card issued by a bank where you have a savings or checking account. The bank may want to dip into your account to collect amounts not paid on your credit-card bill. The bank can do this if it obtains a court order or if you have given the bank permission to make such deductions. (You may have given such permission when you signed the agreement with the bank to obtain your credit card—another example to illustrate the need to read the fine print before signing on the dotted line.)

If you have authorized the bank to automatically deduct from your bank account the amounts you owe on your credit card, and you suspect that a billing error has been made, you can prevent the bank from automatically debiting your account by making sure that the bank receives notice of the billing error within 16 days from the date the billing statement is mailed. Even if you don't write to the bank within this 16-day period, you still have the regular 60-day period to dispute the amount you believe to be in error.

Credit Reports

When you submit an application for a credit card, one of the first things the company will do is obtain a credit report on you. The company will not want to extend credit to you unless the report shows that you are a good credit risk. Frequently the company hires a *consumer reporting agency* to prepare the report on your financial standing. A consumer reporting agency is a business organization which puts together information in your credit file and furnishes this information to a merchant or credit-card issuer for a fee.

The credit file usually contains information about your employment status, the amount of your annual salary, and the number of dependents that you have. In addition, the file usually has information about your credit history, your previous experience with credit-card companies, and your record of making payments. The file can also contain information that is available publicly, such as records of arrests, convictions, tax liens, bankruptcies, and court judgments.

Under the Fair Credit Reporting Act, your file can be disclosed only to someone who plans to use the information for one of the following purposes:

1. To grant you credit or to collect on your credit account.
2. To consider you for possible employment.
3. To determine whether an insurance policy should be issued.
4. To determine whether or not you are eligible for a license or other benefit granted by a government agency which is required by law to consider your financial responsibility and status.
5. In connection with a business transaction between you and another person, as long as the person requesting the report has a legitimate business need for it.
6. In response to a court order.

Your credit file may also be disclosed to someone if you give your written permission to the consumer reporting agency.

The limitation on distribution is quite explicit. Information on a particular consumer may be provided to a third party only if the third party requires it in connection with a specific transaction involving that consumer. In one case, a California company provided merchants with information on the check-cashing histories of thousands of consumers. The court held that this practice was illegal, since merchants who subscribed to the service could not conceivably do business with every individual whose credit information was listed.

Is there any way you can find out what is in your file? If your application for credit is denied by a company because of information supplied by a consumer reporting agency, the company must supply you with the name of the consumer reporting agency. You can find out what information is contained in your file, either by visiting the consumer reporting agency or by telephoning.

If you are simply curious to learn what is in your file, you can contact a consumer reporting agency (although in this case you will probably have to pay a small fee). You can find the names of consumer reporting agencies in your telephone directory under the heading "Credit Reporting Agencies."

To comply with the letter of the law, a reporting agency is supposed to release the information only to persons with proper identification. The agency may establish certain identification procedures for those calling by telephone. For example, if you have been denied credit on the basis of information contained in a credit report, the agency may ask you to mail them a copy of the letter refusing your credit together with a telephone number where you can be reached during the day.

The consumer reporting agency is not required to show you the file itself. Under the law, you are entitled to learn only the "nature and substance" of the information in the file. You do have the right to learn the names of those who have received credit reports on you within the last six months—and the names of those who received credit reports on you within the last two years for employment purposes. You are also entitled to know the sources of the information in your credit file.

If you decide to visit the consumer reporting agency, you can bring along a friend or associate for moral support. As a rule, the agency cannot charge you a fee if you have been refused credit on the basis of information contained in a credit card report and if you ask the agency for information within 30 days of the date you receive notice that credit has been refused.

You may find that the information in your credit file is inaccurate or incomplete. For example, your credit file may contain information to the effect that you were late in paying a certain account when in fact you were not late, or it may state that you never paid a particular bill although you actually did pay it. If this is the case, you should notify the consumer reporting agency immediately. The agency must then reinvestigate the matter (unless it has good reason to believe that the dispute is frivolous or irrelevant). If the reporting agency finds that the information is inaccurate, or that the information can no longer be verified, it must promptly take the information out of your file.

In writing to a consumer reporting agency to request a reinvestigation, you can use a letter similar to the following:

March 1, 1980

Abel Credit Bureau
150 Market Street
Chicago, Illinois

Dear Sir:

On February 25, 1980, I spoke to Mr. Smith at your office and he provided me with the information in my credit file. There is one item of information which is incorrect, and I would like to have you reinvestigate it and correct it.

The item concerns my account with ABC Department Store. You have listed in my file that I failed to pay the sum of $120 and that my account with that store is delinquent. I paid the sum of $120 promptly (see copy of canceled check enclosed herein) and I have never had any problems with my ABC Department Store account. Since the item in my credit file is a mistake, I would appreciate it if you would make a correction as soon as possible.

Very truly yours,
Cathryn Consumer

After reinvestigation, the reporting agency may decide not to change the information or to take it out of your file. You can then file a brief statement describing the nature of your dispute. The consumer reporting agency may limit your statement to 100 words. The advantage of filing a statement is that it tells your side of the story to anyone who later obtains a credit report on you.

The consumer reporting agency must note in any subsequent report that you dispute the information contained in the report, and it must also provide a copy of your statement or a clear and accurate summary of it.

Suppose the inaccurate or incomplete information has already been disclosed to a creditor. The reporting agency is required, at your request, to inform that person of a deletion or change in your file, or of any statement of dispute which you have added.

The law places a time limit on reporting negative information. Consumer reporting agencies can only report information which is no older than seven years, with the exception of bankruptcies, which may be reported if they occurred within the past ten years. Unfavorable information includes items such as past lawsuits, judgments, tax liens, unpaid accounts, and arrest records.

These time limitations do not apply if the credit report is used in connection with a credit transaction involving $50,000 or more, life insurance with a face amount of $50,000 or more, or employment at an annual salary of $20,000 or more.

In rare cases, a company may refuse to extend credit on the basis of information from a source other than a consumer reporting agency. If this happens, you have 60 days to write to the company requesting the reasons for its decision. The company must then disclose the nature of the information to you within a reasonable period of time.

Investigative Reports

If you apply for life or accident insurance, the company reviewing your application may order an *investigative consumer report*. An investigative consumer report differs from an ordinary consumer report in two ways: It contains a different kind of information, and the information is gathered in a different way. While a consumer report contains information relating to your credit history and information available from public records, an investigative report deals with matters of a more personal nature, such as character, general reputation, and life-style. For the most part, the information in an investigative report is obtained by personal interviews with your friends, relatives, and neighbors.

Investigative reports are most often used by insurance companies or institutions granting home mortgages. Potential employers may also use the reports to decide if they want to hire you.

Until recently, very few consumers even knew of these reports. Applicants for insurance were unaware of the fact that their lives were under investigation, or, if they did know of the investigation, they had no knowledge of the true extent of the inquiries made into their personal affairs. In some cases, the agency compiling the investigative report went beyond mere statements about the individual's character and reported instead on his personal activities, hair length, and even sexual habits.

The problems in this area are serious, because they can affect a large number of people. According to *The New Yorker* magazine (April 21, 1975), "Probably fifty million investigative reports on citizens are currently in the files of commercial consumer-investigative agencies, and this number does not include several million investigative reports compiled by large corporations themselves or by private detective agencies specializing in the investigation of people who have applied for employment."

The Fair Credit Reporting Act provides guidelines for companies ordering investigative reports. Under the law, a company does not need to obtain your permission to order an investigative report, but it must notify you within three days after an investigative report has been ordered. This does not apply, however, if the report is to be used for employment purposes in connection with a job for which you have not specifically applied.

Under the law, you are entitled to know the "nature and substance" of all information in your investigative file. But in most cases you are not entitled to know who provided the information. You are entitled to know who has received reports on you within the last six months (or within the last two years if the report was made for employment purposes).

The Fair Credit Reporting Act has not eliminated all of the problems involved in these investigations. Consider this horror story:*

"On December 8, 1971, [William] Stanley, who had various kinds of insurance—on his house, on his automobile, on a boat—with different agents, decided to consolidate his insurance in the hands of a local agency. The agency represented Lumber-

* From "Anything Adverse?" by Thomas Whiteside in the April 21, 1975 issue of *The New Yorker*. Reprinted by permission; © 1975 The New Yorker Magazine, Inc.

mens Mutual Casualty Company, a subsidiary of Kemper Insurance. According to Stanley, his applications for these specific insurance arrangements, including a thirty-five-thousand-dollar policy on his house in New Bern, were accepted, and he received the new policies on December 21, 1971. Shortly thereafter, however, he says, his local agent telephoned with some unwelcome news. The agent said he had been informed by Kemper Insurance that Stanley's application had been investigated and the resulting report was unfavorable . . . and that they were cancelling all of Stanley's insurance policies in the first two weeks of February.

"This news gave Stanley a nasty jolt, and especially so because he could get no further information from his insurance agent. On December 27th, Stanley received a letter from Kemper Insurance formally notifying him that his policies were being cancelled. The only clue to the reason was the rather cryptic observation, 'This action was influenced by information contained in a report made at our request by a nationally known and reputable source of information for business decisions. This source is Retail Credit Co., Wilmington.' Stanley, who was by now extremely upset, telephoned the Retail Credit Company's office in Wilmington, North Carolina, and demanded to see the report. After being required to provide satisfactory information concerning his identity, he was told that he could not see the report, but he was given over the telephone what he says were four items of adverse information from it, relating primarily to his bill-paying record. Stanley vigorously disputed all the adverse information, and demanded a reinvestigation of his standing in the community. But instead of receiving a reversal of the investigative report, Stanley found other misfortunes falling upon him, one after another. He received a letter from the North Carolina Department of Motor Vehicles informing him that, since his insurance company had not sent the bureau a form showing him to possess automobile liability insurance, as North Carolina law required, his car registration was now invalid, and he was ordered to return his license plates. Then he received a letter from the company that held the mortgage on his house notifying him that since his homeowner's insurance policy had been cancelled, he was in default in complying with the terms of his mortgage. Stanley consulted a local attorney, who looked into the Fair Credit Reporting Act and concluded that the act had been violated in that Stanley, in applying for insurance, had not been informed, as the law required, that he might be subject to a consumer-investigation report. On February 1st, Stanley brought a civil suit under the act against Lumbermens Mutual Casualty and Retail Credit, charging that Lumbermens Mutual had cancelled his homeowner's policy on the basis of a Retail Credit investigation that had been illegally undertaken.

"The day after Stanley filed his suit, in a federal court, he received a letter from Retail Credit informing him that the company was not legally required to supply him with a copy of the report on him and would not do so. But someone at Retail Credit had bungled, and Stanley found enclosed with the letter a copy of the very report that the company thought it had refused to supply. According to Stanley, the report rated his 'business, financial or employment reputation' and his 'family reputation or associates' as 'questionable.' It alleged, among other things, that his bill-paying record was not good and that in insurance matters he was 'claims conscious,' and it also asserted that his eighteen-year-old daughter—who Stanley says 'didn't even date at that time'—was 'running freely' with boys.

"If these charges had been made in a report on a poor and uneducated man, his practical chances of remedial action would have been negligible. However, Stanley was neither poor nor uneducated. As it happened, he was the postmaster in New Bern. . . . Because the New Bern Post Office is in a federal building containing a number of other federal offices, to most of which he had access by a master key—Stanley had been subjected to an investigation by the Federal Bureau of Investigation.

"But even these credentials did not slow the momentum of the unfavorable report on Stanley. When, in desperation, Stanley sought to obtain insurance for his house and car from other insurance companies, the agents he approached said that they would not insure him, 'since I had filed a suit against another insurance company.' On top of everything else, Stanley received another letter from the company holding his mortgage, informing him that, owing to the default caused by his continued lack of a homeowner's insurance policy, it intended to begin foreclosure proceedings. Faced with this dire prospect, Stanley appealed to Federal District Judge John D. Larkins for relief, and in response the judge issued a restraining order requiring Kemper Insurance to keep Stanley's homeowner's and automobile insurance in effect pending the outcome of his lawsuit. The lawsuit, which was one of the first suits brought under the Fair Credit

Reporting Act, was settled out of court, and Stanley was eventually able to obtain adequate insurance through an organization that specialized in providing insurance for government employees."

Legal Actions

What remedies do you have if a company violates the law? If a company *intentionally* fails to follow any requirements set out in the Fair Credit Reporting Act, it is liable to you for (1) any actual financial injury which you suffer, (2) any extra penalty which the court sees fit to impose as punishment for intentionally violating the law, and (3) if you win your case in court, court costs and reasonable fees for your attorney. If a company is *negligent* in following the requirements of the law, it is liable to you for any financial injury which you suffer and, if you win your case in court, court costs and reasonable fees for your attorney. In addition, the law provides that anyone obtaining information from a consumer reporting agency under false pretenses is subject to a maximum criminal fine of $5,000 or a maximum of one year in prison, or both.

Discrimination in Credit

In the past, women sometimes had difficulty obtaining credit from banks and retail stores because the officials in charge of credit policies maintained a stereotyped picture of women as "housewives" who had no experience or interest in financial matters. This situation has been changed by passage of the Equal Credit Opportunity Act, which prohibits creditors from discrimination on the basis of sex or marital status. The act also provides that it is illegal to discriminate on the basis of age, religion, race, or national origin.

Under the law, a creditor may not discourage you from applying for credit because of your sex, marital status, age, religion, race, or national origin. In many cases you will be required to fill out an application form to obtain credit. A creditor may not ask you on the form what your sex is. You may be requested to choose a title such as Ms., Miss, Mr., or Mrs. on the application form, but only if the form first tells you that selecting a title is up to you and is not required.

Do you have to disclose your marital status when you apply for credit? The answer to this question depends on whether you are applying for a *secured account*. (In a secured account, you pledge property or collateral to the creditor to secure payment.) If you apply for an *unsecured account*, the creditor may not ask you about your marital status unless you live in a community-property state. You may be asked to supply information about your marital status if you apply for a joint account or a secured account, where you pledge property or collateral to secure payment.

A creditor cannot ask you information about your spouse or former spouse unless:

1. Your spouse is applying with you.
2. Your spouse will be allowed to use your account.
3. You include your spouse's income on the credit-application form.
4. You are relying on alimony or child-support payments from a spouse or former spouse as a basis of repayment.
5. You live in a community-property state or you are relying on property located in a community-property state as a basis for repayment.

A creditor cannot ask you information about birth-control practices or your intentions about having children. However, a creditor may ask you about the number and ages of your dependents or about the financial obligations or expenses you have with respect to these dependents.

In reviewing your application, a creditor must take into consideration all of the income you receive (even part-time employment must be considered if you can demonstrate that the income from this employment is likely to continue). You are *not* required to disclose the amounts received from alimony and child support, but if you do provide this information, the creditor must consider these payments as part of your income if you can show that the payments will be made regularly. Once you make disclosures about alimony or child-support payments, a creditor can ask you for additional information—for example, whether the payments are made pursuant to a court order or a written separation agreement.

Companies sometimes use a "credit scoring system" to review your application. A credit scoring system is a system which evaluates, on the basis of numerical score, an applicant's probable willingness and financial ability to repay the credit requested. The score is based on the applicant's answers to key questions which have been selected and weighted according to the creditor's experience with past applicants.

Once you have submitted a completed application, the creditor must notify you within 30 days of the action it has taken on your application. If your application is accepted, the creditor can notify you of this fact or it can simply send you the credit card or money that you requested in the application. If a creditor rejects your application, it must send you a written notice which contains:

1. A statement of the action it has taken in connection with your application.
2. A statement summarizing the provisions of the Equal Credit Opportunity Act.
3. The name and address of the federal agency that administers compliance with the act.
4. A statement of the specific reasons for the action taken—or a notice that you have 60 days to request such a statement. This notice must contain the name, address, and telephone number of the person from whom you can obtain this information.

If your application is rejected, the creditor must give you the *specific reasons* for the decision. The creditor cannot merely state that you were refused credit on the basis of "internal standards" or because you failed to obtain a high enough score on the credit scoring system.

You can file a lawsuit in federal court against any creditor who violates your rights under the Equal Credit Opportunity Act. If you win your case, you may recover any actual damages which you sustained, and you may also obtain punitive damages up to $10,000. In addition, you can be reimbursed for court costs and attorney's fees.

If you think that a creditor has violated the law, you may be able to obtain help from the federal government. Several agencies are responsible for making sure that the Equal Credit Opportunity Act is enforced. If you are denied credit, the creditor is required to furnish you with the name and address of the specific agency which has jurisdiction over the creditor.

Employment Discrimination

Cynthia Di Salvo filed a charge of sex discrimination against her employer because she was paid less than several male employees with comparable responsibility.

Ms. Di Salvo was employed by the Chamber of Commerce of Greater Kansas City, an organization formed to promote community development and enhance the local economy. The Chamber of Commerce issued a monthly publication called *The Kansas City Magazine*.

In 1972, Ms. Di Salvo was hired as an associate editor of the magazine at an annual salary of $7,800. Several months later she received a raise to $8,200 a year, but she discovered that two male employees, recently hired by the Chamber of Commerce, were making much more money. One was earning $12,000 a year, the other $11,000.

When she realized that there was little hope of receiving a substantial salary increase, she filed a charge of sex discrimination against the Chamber of Commerce. A few months later, she resigned her position as associate editor to take a job with an advertising agency. After she resigned, the Chamber of Commerce hired a male employee to serve as a "communications specialist" at an annual salary of $12,000.

At the trial, the court found that Ms. Di Salvo performed duties which were "substantially equal" to those performed by her male successor, although her salary was $3,800 a year less than his. The court also determined that the two other male employees in her department were paid more money than she received, although their work involved no more skill, effort or responsibility than Ms. Di Salvo's.

The court concluded that the Chamber of Commerce had discriminated against her on the basis of sex and awarded her $13,808 in back pay.

Employment discrimination like that in the case described above can be challenged under Title VII of the Civil Rights Act of 1964. Congress enacted Title VII to assure equality of employment opportunities by eliminating those practices that discriminate on the basis of race, color, religion, sex, or national origin.

According to the Supreme Court, "Congress did not intend by Title VII, however, to guarantee a job to every person regardless of qualifications. . . . What is required by Congress is the removal of artificial, arbitrary, and unnecessary barriers to employment when the barriers operate invidiously to discriminate on the basis of racial or other impermissible classification."

Under the Civil Rights Act, the courts may issue an injunction against an employer to stop discriminatory practices and order the employer to take whatever affirmative action may be appropriate to remedy the effects of past unlawful employment practices.

Discriminatory Practices

Under the provisions of Title VII, you cannot be denied a job or fair treatment on a job because of discrimination. The Act provides that you can file an action against an employer who discriminates with regard to:

1. Hiring or firing.
2. Compensation or salary terms.
3. Transfer, promotion, layoff, and recall.
4. Use of company facilities.
5. Training and apprenticeship programs.
6. Fringe benefits such as health insurance, retirement plans, and disability payments.
7. Employment references.
8. All other terms and conditions of employment.

It is also unlawful for an employer to limit, segregate, or classify his employees or applicants for employment in any way which would deprive any individual of employment opportunities or otherwise adversely affect his or her status as an employee.

A discrimination charge under Title VII can be brought against any employer who has fifteen or more employees. This includes most major corporations, banks, and educational institutions.

However, if you work for a small business or a professional who employs only a handful of people, you do not have any recourse under this law. Employers covered by Title VII are required to post in a conspicuous place a notice giving summaries of the law and information about the filing of charges.

The law has special provisions dealing with federal employees and applicants for federal jobs. These employees are protected under guidelines administered by the Civil Service Commission which prohibit job discrimination based on race, color, sex, religion, or national origin. Federal workers may file private lawsuits if discrimination charges are not settled satisfactorily within the government agency or the Civil Service Commission.

Title VII also has an exemption for national-security posts. It is not an unlawful employment practice for an employer to fail or refuse to hire an individual if employment in the position is subject to any requirement imposed in the interest of national security of the United States. This is why, with all the news of undercover activities by the CIA, you have yet to read about any charge of sex or race discrimination filed by a "secret agent."

Many people obtain their jobs by submitting an application to an employment agency. A claim under Title VII may be filed against an employment agency if it discriminates in placing classified advertisements or referring applicants for employment. An employment agency that receives a job order containing an unlawful sex specification will share responsibility with the employer placing the job order if the agency fills the order knowing that the sex specification is not based upon a valid and compelling business reason.

A claim under Title VII may also be filed against a labor union with fifteen or more members. The law provides that a union may not discriminate with regard to applications for membership, referrals for employment, and training and apprenticeship programs. A union may also be liable under the provisions of this law if it causes or attempts to cause an employer to discriminate.

How to File a Discrimination Charge

If you believe that you have been discriminated against in an employment situation because of your race, color, sex, religion, or place of national origin, you may file a lawsuit under Title VII.

Before you commence the suit, however, you *must* first file a complaint with the Equal Employment Opportunity Commission (EEOC), which has authority to investigate claims of discrimination. The language of Title VII makes it clear that you must comply with certain procedural requirements when filing a complaint. The procedural requirements are remarkably complex. One judge has stated that they are "sufficiently labyrinthine to baffle the most experienced lawyer," let alone the layman. The most important provisions of the law concern the time periods in which a charge must be filed.

The time provisions vary somewhat depending on whether or not the complaint is made in a state or locality that has an antidiscrimination law and an agency empowered to enforce that law.

1. When an unlawful employment practice occurs in a state or city which does not have its own antidiscrimination law, the complaint must be filed with the Equal Employment Opportunity Commission within 180 *days* of the discriminatory act.

2. When an unlawful employment practice occurs in a state or city which *does* have its own antidiscrimination law, the person wishing to file a complaint must wait to do so until 60 *days* after commencing proceedings under the state or local law. In other words, the individual must first file a discrimination charge with the state or local agency within the time period required by that agency. Then after waiting 60 days, he can file the complaint with the Equal Employment Opportunity Commission. In all such cases, the charge must be filed with the EEOC *no more than 300 days* after the occurrence of the discriminatory act or within 30 days after receipt of notice that the state or local agency has terminated its proceeding, whichever comes first.

As a practical matter, it is usually best to file charges simultaneously with the state agency and the EEOC. This is done by informing EEOC of the simultaneous filing and requesting that, 60 days from receipt of the charge, the EEOC automatically assume jurisdiction.

The EEOC now has district offices in thirty-two cities across the country. Employees of the agency will give you information about the provisions of Title VII and will answer questions about the time periods for filing discrimination charges. To protect your legal rights, you should file a charge as soon as possible. If you file after the required time, you may not be able to obtain a hearing despite the merits of your case.

There have been some unusual cases in which the time periods have been suspended. In one such case, a woman was hired by an Atlanta firm to serve as the director of its newly established consumer-services project. After several months, she was notified by letter that she could not be retained because of a "limitation of funds." Six months later she learned for the first time that the position of director of consumer services had subsequently been filled by a less-qualified male employee. When she learned of her replacement, she immediately filed charges of sex discrimination with the EEOC. The employer argued that the case should be dismissed, since the woman had not filed charges within the required time. A federal court decided that the filing was proper since the time period did not begin to run until the facts that would support a charge of discrimination under Title VII were apparent or should have been apparent to a person with a reasonably prudent regard for his rights.

An employee may also be able to get around the time limitations in Title VII if he can show that there has been a "continuing violation" of the law. Realistically, however, there are few acts of employment discrimination which fall within this category. As one court observed, "Once a disparaging remark is made, or a transfer is denied, or a demeaning work assignment is given, or indeed an application for employment is rejected, it is, without more, a complete and isolated act; such practices—however long-lasting their repercussions may appear from the subjective viewpoint of the aggrieved [employee]—do not give the [employee] a perpetual right to file charges before the EEOC."

If you file a discrimination charge with the EEOC, you will be asked to complete a form like the one on pages 122–123. Unless there are special circumstances, you will probably have to complete the form at an EEOC office. You do not have to hire a lawyer to file a charge with the EEOC. But you should be careful to make the charge as complete as possible and to list all of the parties (including labor unions or employment agencies) who were involved in the discriminatory practices.

Once the charge has been filed, the EEOC will send notice to all of the parties named in the complaint. The EEOC will then conduct an investigation to determine if the charge has merit under the law. If the investigation reveals sufficient evidence of discrimination, the EEOC's findings will be reported to all parties and attempts will be made to resolve the dispute through informal methods of conciliation. The case will be closed if all the parties arc able to agree on a settlement. If a settlement is not reached, the EEOC may file suit in Federal District Court on your behalf.

If, however, the EEOC does not obtain sufficient evidence of discrimination, the agency will terminate its investigation. The EEOC will then send you a *right-to-sue letter*, informing you that you have a right to sue the employer in Federal District Court. If you receive such a letter from the EEOC, *you must file suit within 90 days*.

The EEOC has a heavy backlog of cases, and it may take some time for the agency to review your complaint. If you wish to proceed to federal court at the earliest possible time rather than wait for the EEOC to investigate your complaint, you can request that the EEOC send you a right-to-sue letter. This request can be made at any time after EEOC has had jurisdiction of the case for *180 days*, even if the EEOC has not opened your file or attempted to conciliate among the parties.

Remember that if you receive a right-to-sue letter from the EEOC, you must begin your lawsuit within 90 days. The federal judge hearing the case will consider any findings made by the EEOC, but basically he will make his own determination of the facts. This means that you can prevail in federal court even if the EEOC has previously determined that there is no basis for your claim.

You can bring an action in federal court without an attorney. Usually, a person who files his own lawsuit is said to appear "pro se," or on his own behalf. In most federal courts, there is a special "pro se" clerk who will help you file the complaint and will answer questions about court procedure.

Realistically speaking, your chances will be substantially improved if you retain an attorney. An attorney who is familiar with the provisions of Title VII will make certain that all of the necessary allegations are included in the complaint and that all procedural requirements are met. The best time to find an attorney is *before* you request a right-to-sue letter from the EEOC. Once you receive a right-to-sue letter, you will have only 90 days to file suit, and most attorneys prefer to have more time to investigate the case and prepare legal papers.

You may be able to find an attorney with expertise in this area by contacting your local bar association's referral service. You may also be able to obtain the name of a qualified attorney from the EEOC, or if the case involves sex discrimination, from a women's-rights organization. Most attorneys charge a fee for this

(PLEASE PRINT OR TYPE)

APPROVED BY GAO		CHARGE NUMBER(S) (AGENCY USE ONLY)
B—180541 (RO510) Expires 1-31-81	CHARGE OF DISCRIMINATION IMPORTANT: This form is affected by the Privacy Act of 1974; see Privacy Act Statement on reverse before completing it.	☐ EEOC

Equal Employment Opportunity Commission

NAME (Indicate Mr., Ms. or Mrs.) _____ HOME TELEPHONE NUMBER (Include area code)

STREET ADDRESS _____

CITY, STATE, AND ZIP CODE _____ COUNTY

NAMED IS THE EMPLOYER, LABOR ORGANIZATION, EMPLOYMENT AGENCY, APPRENTICESHIP COMMITTEE, STATE OR LOCAL GOVERNMENT AGENCY WHO DISCRIMINATED AGAINST ME. (If more than one list below).

NAME _____ TELEPHONE NUMBER (Include area code)

STREET ADDRESS _____ CITY, STATE, AND ZIP CODE

NAME _____ TELEPHONE NUMBER (Include area code)

STREET ADDRESS _____ CITY, STATE, AND ZIP CODE

CAUSE OF DISCRIMINATION BASED ON MY (Check appropriate box(es))

☐ RACE   ☐ COLOR   ☐ SEX   ☐ RELIGION   ☐ NATIONAL ORIGIN   ☐ OTHER (Specify)

DATE MOST RECENT OR CONTINUING DISCRIMINATION TOOK
PLACE *(Month, day, and year)*

THE PARTICULARS ARE:

I will advise the agency if I change my address or telephone number and I will cooperate fully with it in the processing of my charge in accordance with its procedures.

I declare under penalty of perjury that the foregoing is true and correct.

DATE: CHARGING PARTY (Signature)

work, but bear in mind that under the provisions of Title VII you may be able to recover attorney's fees from the other side if you win the suit.

How to Prove Discrimination

A person who files a claim under Title VII has the burden of proving the employer engaged in discriminatory practices. To establish a case, certain general requirements must be met. A person alleging racial discrimination under Title VII must usually show:

1. That he belongs to a racial minority.
2. That he applied for and was qualified for a job for which the employer was seeking applicants.
3. That, despite his qualifications, he was rejected.
4. That after his rejection, his position remained open and the employer continued to seek applications from persons with the same qualifications.

Once the applicant establishes these facts, the burden then shifts to the employer to articulate some legitimate, nondiscriminatory reason for the applicant's rejection. However, the inquiry does not end there. The applicant may still be able to prove that the employer's stated reason for rejection was in fact a pretext.

An action under Title VII can be maintained when there is evidence of overt discrimination—or when there is proof that the employer's policies have a *discriminatory impact*. Employment practices or procedures which seem to be neutral cannot be maintained if they operate to "freeze" the status quo of prior discriminatory practices.

In some cases a black or minority applicant may be able to support his claim by using statistical evidence. The applicant may be able to show that there is a statistical disparity between the proportion of blacks in the employer's work force and the proportion of blacks in the relevant labor market. In these cases, the court may consider the employer's intent or motivation, but good intentions will not justify the use of employment practices that have a discriminatory impact on minority groups.

Employment discrimination can take place not only in the

blue-collar sector, but at the executive level as well. The only difference is that discrimination at the upper levels may be more subtle. An employer in a profession which traditionally has been white may gauge a minority-group applicant against the white stereotype and conclude that he lacks certain "intangible qualities" which are needed for the position. Some companies do not even advertise to fill these positions, but use word-of-mouth recruiting by their own employees. A policy of referral by all-white employees may be a violation of Title VII because of its tendency to perpetuate the homogeneous composition of the work force.

Many of the claims filed under Title VII are based on the theory that the employer's policies have a discriminatory impact on black and other minority applicants. In one case, a minority job applicant challenged an employer's decision to reject all new applicants with less than honorable discharges from military service. To support his case, the applicant cited a government survey showing that minority service members receive a higher proportion of general and undesirable discharges than nonminority members of similar aptitude and education. The applicant was thus able to show that the employer's policy had a discriminatory impact on minority groups.

When a practice is found to have a discriminatory impact, it can be justified only by showing that it is required by *business necessity*. The employer must show that the practice is related to job performance, that it effectively carries out the purpose it is supposed to serve, and that there are no alternative policies or practices which would serve the same purpose with less discriminatory impact.

The Supreme Court has ruled on several cases in which the employer has argued that his policies were justified by "business necessity." In one case, three black employees challenged the educational and testing requirements used by a North Carolina firm. The firm had a policy of hiring and promoting only those persons who had high school diplomas or who had scored well in certain intelligence tests.

The Supreme Court ruled that these requirements could not be justified by "business necessity," since there was no proof that they were related to job performance. The court noted that there was evidence that the employer's policies affected a larger number of black applicants than white. The court found that the requirements of a diploma and intelligence testing, although racially neutral on their face, did in fact discriminate against blacks

in that the requirements rendered ineligible a markedly disproportionate number of blacks.

The Supreme Court concluded that it would not allow employment policies "that operate as 'built-in headwinds' for minority
groups and are unrelated to measuring job capability."

Sex Discrimination

Although progress has been made in recent years, it is clear
that women have still not attained equal standing with men in
the business world. Statistics show that the median pay of women
workers in the U.S. is $8,227 a year, only 60% of the $13,693
median pay of men. In large part, this disparity stems from traditional attitudes and prejudices that have channeled women into
low-paying jobs, such as clerical and secretarial work. As long as
this situation continues, women will have to resort to the provisions of Title VII to obtain equal treatment.

The statute provides that it is an unlawful employment practice
to fail or refuse to hire any person, or to discriminate against any
person with respect to compensation or terms of employment,
because of that person's sex. Under the law, a charge can be filed
against an employer who has a policy of hiring only male applicants.

In one recent case, a female teacher applied for a position at a
new school after the administrators had decided that they wanted
to fill the position with a man. The teacher testified that she had
a solid academic background and that her performance had always been rated satisfactory by her superiors. She claimed that
when she applied for the new position she was told by the principal that there were too many women in the school. The court
ruled that the school administrators had not given fair consideration to her application and had engaged in discriminatory hiring
practices.

The law prohibits discrimination *on the basis of sex*. However,
employers are apparently free to discriminate between different
classes of women on the basis of physical attributes.

In one case, a woman claimed that she had been fired from
her job as a cocktail waitress because she was small-breasted. The
State Appeals Board found that she had been terminated because

her figure made it impossible to wear the required costume. The board held that the employer's decision to discharge the waitress did not constitute sex discrimination. In a similar case, a woman claimed that she lost her job as a Playboy Bunny because she no longer possessed the "Bunny image." The evidence indicated that she was terminated because she had reached "that physiological transition from that youthful fresh look to the womanly look." The State Appeals Board held that the actions of the Playboy Club did not constitute sex discrimination.

Secretaries and other office workers frequently complain about the "sexist" demands of their employers. In one case, a female secretary refused to wash coffee cups or make coffee in preparation for executive meetings. The court ruled that the employer who imposed these conditions had not violated the provisions of Title VII. The court's reasoning was that since the work duties required all secretaries to make coffee, the requirement did not constitute sex discrimination.

Women sometimes have to tolerate "little jokes" and sexual innuendo from their co-workers. The situation is far more serious, however, when a woman is told by her employer that she must submit to his sexual demands or lose her job.

In one case, a woman alleged that she was employed as a secretary under the direction of a male supervisor. The supervisor told her that she should have lunch with him in order to discuss his upcoming evaluation of her work, as well as a possible job promotion. At lunch, he made advances toward her, indicating his desire to have sexual relations with her and stating that this would be necessary if they were to have a satisfactory working relationship. When the woman attempted to leave the restaurant, the supervisor responded first by threats of recrimination against her and then by threats of physical force. During the dispute, he told her that no one at the company would help her if she lodged a complaint against him. On the following day, she stated that she wanted to leave the company as a result of the incident. She agreed to continue work only after she was promised a transfer to another position elsewhere in the company. A comparable position was not found, however, and she was placed in an inferior position in another department. Eventually she was fired.

A federal court ruled that a charge of sex discrimination could be made based upon these allegations. The court stated that there is a violation of Title VII whenever a supervisor, with the actual or constructive knowledge of the employer, makes sexual advances or demands toward a subordinate employee and conditions that employee's job, status, promotion, and other aspects of career development on a favorable response to those advances or demands.

Some companies require women applicants to provide detailed information about their personal lives. Questions about marital status, pregnancy, and future childbearing plans are frequently used to discriminate against women and may be a violation of Title VII if used to deny or limit employment opportunities for women applicants.

Some employers have established minimum height and weight requirements for applicants. These requirements may be illegal if they screen out a disproportionate number of women and have no direct relationship to the job in question.

Of course, male applicants can also bring discrimination charges under Title VII. In one unusual case, three male actors filed a complaint against the Los Angeles Rams because they were not given a chance to try out for the team's cheerleading squad called the "Embraceable Ewes." The actors maintained that the club had engaged in sex discrimination. They argued that cheering is "not a thing to show your legs, it's to rouse spirit."

Even in an obvious case of discrimination, the employer has a legal defense if he can show that sex is a *bona fide occupational qualification reasonably necessary to the normal operation of the business*. The test is one of business necessity. An employer cannot refuse to hire an individual simply because his employees prefer to work with a member of their own sex.

In one case, a young man applied for a job as a flight cabin attendant with Pan American Airlines. He was rejected because Pan Am had a policy of hiring only women for that position. The company maintained that the performance of female attendants was better in such nonmechanical aspects of the job as "providing reassurance to anxious passengers, giving courteous personalized service and, in general, making flights as pleasurable as possible within the limitations imposed by aircraft operations." The company even offered evidence to show that passengers overwhelmingly preferred to be served by female stewardesses.

Nevertheless, the court found that these factors did not justify Pan Am's policy. The court pointed out that the primary function of an airline is to transport passengers safely from one point to another. There was no evidence to show that hiring male flight attendants would so seriously affect the operation of the airline as to jeopardize or even reduce its ability to provide safe transportation. The court noted that "discrimination based on sex is valid only when the *essence* of the business operation would be undermined by not hiring members of one sex exclusively."

Religious Discrimination

What happens when an employee is obligated to work on Saturday, but his religious beliefs prevent him from working on that day?

EEOC guidelines provide that an employer has an obligation "to make reasonable accommodations to the religious needs of employees and prospective employees where such accommodations can be made without undue hardship on the conduct of the employer's business." It is not clear, however, exactly what constitutes "undue hardship."

Recently the Supreme Court was asked to determine the extent of an employer's obligation to accommodate an employee whose religious beliefs prohibited him from working on Saturdays. The employee in that case was hired by TWA to work in its Kansas City stores department. TWA maintained that the stores department had to operate twenty-four hours a day, 365 days a year. Whenever an employee's job in that department was not filled, the company had to bring in an employee from another department or assign a supervisor to cover the job.

In the spring of 1968, the employee began to study a religion known as the Worldwide Church of God. One of the tenets of that religion is that one must observe the Sabbath by refraining from performing any work from sunset on Friday to sunset on Saturday.

There was no serious conflict until the employee bid for and received a transfer from Building 1, where he had been employed, to Building 2, where he worked the day shift. The two buildings had entirely separate seniority lists, and while in Building 1 the employee had sufficient seniority to observe the Sabbath regularly, he was second from the bottom on the Building 2 seniority list.

In Building 2 the employee was asked to work Saturdays when a fellow employee went on vacation. The company agreed to consider a change of work assignments for the employee, but the union was not willing to violate the seniority provisions set out in its collective-bargaining contract, and the employee had insufficient seniority to bid for a shift having Saturdays off.

The dispute came to a head when the employee refused to report for work on Saturdays. A hearing was held and the employee was discharged on grounds of insubordination for refusing to work during his designated shift.

The Supreme Court ruled that TWA had made reasonable efforts to accommodate the employee. The court noted that Title VII does not require an employer to carve out a special exception to its seniority system in order to accommodate an employee's religious practices.

The Spoils of Victory

When you win an employment-discrimination suit, you can obtain substantial compensation.

If the court finds that the employer has intentionally engaged in an unlawful employment practice, the court may enjoin, or prohibit, the employer from engaging in the unlawful practice, and order such action as may be appropriate under the circumstances. Specifically, the court may grant you the following relief:

1. If your application for employment has been rejected for improper reasons, the court may require the employer to hire you. If you have been discharged from a position in violation of the law, the court may order the employer to reinstate you to your original position with full seniority.

2. The court may award you "back pay" to compensate you for lost wages. The time for computing this back pay begins two years prior to the date when charges were filed with the EEOC. The court can reduce the total award by any amounts which you earned—or could have earned with reasonable diligence—in other employment.

3. The court may award you attorney's fees and court costs. (In one case, a federal court determined that an award of $11,500 for attorney's fees was appropriate.)

4. The court may order the employer to make contributions to group life insurance and medical plans for the period in question.

5. The court may order the employer to remove false or adverse material from your file.

6. In class actions, or cases involving numerous employees, the court may order the employer to engage in broad affirmative-action programs. For example, the employer may have to initiate special training programs for blacks or other minorities deprived of their rights.

If you lose the case, however, you may be required to pay the employer's attorney's fees. The court can award attorney's fees to an employer whenever it finds that the complaint is unreasonable or frivolous, or was maintained after it was evident there was no case.

If you want to sue your employer simply to "get back" at him or cause him embarrassment, you should consider the possible costs. But if you are convinced that you have a legitimate claim, by all means go ahead.

Additional Help

It is important to note that employees are also protected by other federal laws.

The Equal Pay Act makes it illegal for an employer to pay a woman less than a man if she is doing the same work under the same conditions requiring the same skill, effort, and responsibility. A woman manager working for Pizza Hut was able to recover damages under this law when she proved she was the lowest-paid unit manager in the area and earned an average salary of $735 per month, which was $100 less than the average for all male managers.

There is now a federal act which prohibits discrimination in employment with respect to persons between the ages of forty and seventy years. Under the act, it is illegal to refuse to hire or to discharge any person because of that person's age—unless the employer can show that age is "a bona fide occupational qualification" reasonably necessary to the normal operation of the business. Two officials of the Little Rock Fire Department filed suit under this law, claiming that they had been forced into retirement at the age of sixty-two. The city maintained that age was a factor in job performance, but the court found no basis for the city's claim outside of mere stereotyping of older workers as being unable to "cut the mustard." The court held that the two officials were entitled to reinstatement as well as back pay.

The Fourteenth Amendment of the Constitution guarantees all persons equal protection under the law. The best example of an employment-discrimination claim based on the Fourteenth Amendment is the famous Yankee locker-room case in which a woman reporter for *Sports Illustrated* filed suit against the Commissioner of Baseball and the New York Yankees, claiming that she had been barred from the club's locker room after a World Series game.

The reporter claimed that the ban prevented her from doing her job properly and placed her at a competitive disadvantage. She noted that the best stories often come from comments made by the players immediately after the game or during special question-and-answer sessions in the locker room.

The Baseball Commissioner and the Yankees claimed that the policy was necessary "to protect and preserve the national image of baseball as a family game . . . and to preserve baseball's audience and to maintain its popularity and standing." The team also claimed that the policy was needed to protect the privacy of players who were undressing or getting ready to shower. The judge was not persuaded by these arguments and pointed out that the club could install curtains or swinging doors to protect the players' privacy and "to shield them from the roving eyes of female reporters."

The judge held that the reasons advanced were not sufficient to defeat the constitutional rights of the woman reporter. The court issued an order preventing the club from excluding women reporters from the locker room and requiring it to adopt other means of preserving player privacy.

Affirmative Action

In recent years a number of major companies have established affirmative-action programs to increase the number of minority workers hired or considered for promotion to higher-level positions. Some companies have even developed special training or apprenticeship programs for minority applicants. Supporters of affirmative action claim that employers should be encouraged to set up goals or timetables for hiring minority workers to correct the harmful effects of past discrimination. Opponents, on the other hand, maintain that employment goals are really "quotas" for hiring a specified number of persons from one group, and that affirmative-action programs constitute "reverse discrimination."

In 1974, a white lab technician named Brian Weber challenged an affirmative-action program set up by Kaiser Aluminum in its Louisiana plant. Weber complained that Kaiser used a quota system to select employees for training programs and gave preferential treatment to minority workers in violation of Title VII.

Kaiser set up its affirmative-action program to comply with a Presidential order which required companies doing business with the federal government not only to refrain from discrimination, but to take affirmative action to correct racial imbalance. To comply with the order, the company restructured its crafts-training program. Eligibility for training still rested on plant seniority, but to implement the affirmative-action goal, the company set up dual seniority lists: for each two training vacancies, one black and one white employee were selected on the basis of seniority within their respective racial groups.

Brian Weber's application for the training program was rejected, although some black employees—with less seniority—were admitted to the program. Weber charged that the program was "reverse discrimination," which he claimed was not permitted under the provisions of Title VII.

The Supreme Court held, however, that Kaiser's voluntary affirmative-action plan did not violate the law. The court noted that Kaiser's plan and the provisions of Title VII were both designed "to break down old patterns of racial segregation and hierarchy. Both were structured to 'open employment opportunities for Negroes in occupations which have been traditionally closed to them.'

"At the same time the plan does not necessarily trammel the interests of the white employees. The plan does not require the discharge of white workers and their replacement with new black workers. Nor does the plan create an absolute bar to the advancement of white employees; half of those trained in the program will be white."

The court concluded that the adoption of the Kaiser plan "falls within the area of discretion left by Title VII to the private sector voluntarily to adopt affirmative action plans to eliminate conspicuous racial imbalance in traditionally segregated job categories."

9

Bankruptcy

Most people today are engaged in a fierce and continuing struggle to maintain their financial balance. Somehow—despite the easy credit and high interest rates, despite the inflation and enticements to spend—most people succeed.

But every once in a while, the struggle is lost. Some people try their best, but are never quite able to cut their expenses to match their income, or raise their income to meet their expenses. So they go into debt. Trying to close the gap, they work a little harder, shop a little more carefully, cut out the luxuries, even trim some of the essentials, but it is not enough. And then a catastrophe strikes—the loss of a job, a serious illness or accident, the breakup of a marriage—and finally they have reached their limit. Bill collectors pound on the door and call on the telephone, the electric company threatens to turn off the power, the bank wants to repossess the car . . . and there is no relief in sight.

Or so it may seem. The truth is, however, that there is a source of relief, and every year almost 200,000 people take advantage of it. That source of relief is the declaration of bankruptcy.

Deciding Whether to Declare Bankruptcy

Before you decide to file for bankruptcy, you should consider speaking to a consumer counseling service. These services, located in most major cities, are often able to help people plan a budget, have payment schedules adjusted on department-store and other charge accounts, and in a number of other ways help people rearrange their financial affairs so as to avoid bankruptcy.

However, when a person's financial situation finally becomes unmanageable and is on the verge of complete collapse, filing for bankruptcy is a way of heading off that final disaster and of protecting as much of one's remaining possessions as possible. This is done by the court's taking a person's assets (except for certain important possessions exempted by law) and using them to pay off—usually only partially—that person's debts. When creditors receive only partial payment, the remainder of the debt is considered "discharged" by the court. The person who has declared bankruptcy is thereby given a clean slate and an opportunity to continue to function in society, but without the crushing burden of excessive debt.

There are still some people who consider it disgraceful to declare bankruptcy, but it is certainly nothing to be ashamed of. It is simply a legal procedure which enables the debtor to "write off" certain payments which he can no longer meet. And if its use is acceptable for such corporate giants as REA Express or W.T. Grant, on whose boards sat pillars of American business, you should not hesitate to use it when it is to your advantage to do so. That's why the law is there.

Most people believe that it is necessary to hire a lawyer to assist them in filing for bankruptcy. As a rule, lawyers usually charge a fee of $200 to $800 for this service. Perhaps that's one of the reasons why people who have some money are more likely to file for bankruptcy than people who are desperately poor. Convinced that a lawyer is necessary, the poor often find themselves *too* poor to declare bankruptcy. Fortunately, however, filing for bankruptcy is a relatively simple procedure, consisting of filling out half a dozen forms, filing them with the clerk of the bankruptcy court, and making one or two brief appearances in court. (There is a filing fee of $60, but with the filing of a special form, permission can be obtained to pay the fee in installments). Even if you retain a lawyer, you will still have to provide detailed answers to all of the questions on the form. So it is often more convenient and more economical to do it yourself.

This chapter concerns individual petitions for *voluntary* bankruptcy, which are petitions filed by individual persons to obtain a discharge of their debts. (When a petition is filed by the creditors demanding payment, the proceeding is called an *involuntary* bankruptcy.)

The information in this chapter is not designed to help people who own or operate their own businesses. These individuals should consult with an attorney before filing a petition in bankruptcy court.

Necessary Forms

Since bankruptcy court is part of the federal court system, the forms and procedures for filing are essentially the same throughout the country. To file for bankruptcy you will need the following forms:

1. Petition for Voluntary Bankruptcy
2. Statement of Affairs
3. Statement of All Liabilities
4. Statement of All Property
5. Summary of Debts and Property
6. List of Creditors

If you must pay your filing fee in installments, you will need a seventh form, an Application to Pay Filing Fees in Installments.

The more widely used legal forms, including bankruptcy forms, are generally available in well-supplied stationery stores. Bankruptcy forms are usually sold as a complete set, which should include at least five copies of each of the seven forms. (Some sets do not include the List of Creditors or Application to Pay Filing Fees in Installments, in which case you will have to purchase them separately.) You will file an original and three copies with the clerk of the court, and retain a copy for your own files.

If you are married and you plan to file for bankruptcy, will your spouse have to file, too? The answer is no. But remember that many debts and obligations are incurred by both the husband and the wife. Contracts to purchase automobiles and appliances, for example, are often signed by both persons. If only one person is discharged from the debt by filing a petition in bankruptcy, the other may still be open to suit.

If you wish, you and your spouse can file a joint petition. The court will then decide whether the property owned by you and your spouse should be consolidated for purposes of the bankruptcy proceeding.

Samples of some of the forms that you will have to file are printed at the end of this chapter.

Petition for Voluntary Bankruptcy. This form requires little more than your name and address. By its use, you are petitioning for relief as a voluntary bankrupt and are swearing that all the statements in your filing are true to the best of your knowledge.

Statement of Affairs. Filling out this form provides the court with an overview of your affairs: name and address, occupation and income, taxes recently refunded or paid, bank accounts, financial records, and other matters pertaining to your financial affairs. Simply answer the questions factually to the best of your ability.

Statement of All Liabilities. On this form, you must list *all* of your debts, including debts to friends and relatives. You will divide them into three categories: Creditors Having Priority, Creditors Holding Security, and Creditors Having Unsecured Claims Without Priority.

1. Debts owed to "creditors having priority" are placed in a special category. They include wages and commissions due to someone in your employ, and taxes due to the federal, state, and city government. A creditor having priority is in a favored position if there are any assets to be distributed.

2. Debts owed to "creditors holding security" refers to those debts for which you have signed agreements specifying that certain of your possessions will serve as security until the debts are paid in full. For example, if you purchased an automobile "on time," you probably signed a sales agreement that specified not only the price of the car and the amount of the monthly payments, but also that the car would serve as security until you paid in full. Through bankruptcy you will be relieved of the burden of paying off all such secured debts, but your creditors will have the right to reclaim the security. In other words, you will not have to make the remaining monthly payments, but the car dealer can repossess the car. Before you file for bankruptcy, you should review all of your contracts and sales agreements to determine which creditors have a security interest in your property.

3. Debts "owed to creditors having unsecured claims without priority" refers to all other debts that do not fall into the previous two categories—that is, debts that you have incurred without putting up security or collateral. Generally, this would include debts owed to credit-card companies, department stores, doctors, lawyers, electric and gas companies, friends, and relatives.

Statement of All Property. On this form you must list all of your property, divided into four categories: Real Property, Personal Property, Property Not Otherwise Scheduled, and Property Claimed as Exempt.

1. "Real property" refers to any interest or ownership you may have in real estate—that is, in land or buildings. If you own a home or have any holdings in land, you should consult an attorney before filing for bankruptcy.

2. The Statement of All Property lists twenty-two kinds of "personal property," such as cash, bank deposits, household goods, wearing apparel and jewelry, vehicles, livestock, farm supplies and machinery, office equipment, inventory, etc.

3. "Property not otherwise scheduled" refers to any kinds of property not included in the first two categories.

4. "Property claimed as exempt" is an important category because it refers to those items from among all your possessions that are exempt from being used to pay off your creditors. The purpose of the bankruptcy procedure is not, after all, to reduce you to abject poverty, but to enable you to get a new start. Consequently, provision is made in the bankruptcy law for you to retain a certain number of possessions.

Until recently, each state had its own list of exemptions. When the new federal bankruptcy law went into effect on October 1, 1979, however, the procedure for selecting exemptions became more complicated. Before the new law was passed, there was considerable debate in Congress about whether there should be an exclusive list of federal exemptions or whether the exemptions should be determined by each individual state. The final bill passed by Congress contains a compromise. It provides that the debtor may select either the federal exemptions or the exemptions provided by state law. However, it also provides that the individual states may enact legislation precluding the debtor from selecting the federal exemptions.

In practice, this means that if you plan to file a petition for bankruptcy, you can select either the federal exemptions or the state exemptions, unless your state has passed a law preventing you from selecting the federal exemptions.

The federal exemptions include the following:

1. Real property or personal property that the debtor uses as a residence (this includes a mobile home), not to exceed $7,500 in value.

2. A motor vehicle, not to exceed $1,200 in value.

3. Household goods, wearing apparel, appliances, books, animals, crops, or musical instruments, not to exceed $200 in value for any particular item.
4. Jewelry, not to exceed $500 in value.
5. Professional books or tools of a trade, not to exceed $750 in value.
6. Any unmatured life-insurance policy owned by the debtor (other than a credit life-insurance policy).
7. Social security, veteran's or disability benefits, alimony, or support, maintenance up to an amount reasonably necessary for the support of the debtor and any dependent of the debtor.
8. An additional "wild card" exemption of $400, plus any unused amount in the exemption provided in paragraph 1, which may be applied to any other property.

The last provision can be very helpful. Suppose you have jewelry worth $1,500. Under paragraph (4) you are only entitled to an exemption of $500. But this provision allows you to add another $400, plus any *unused amount* under paragraph (1). So all of your jewelry, worth $1,500, can be exempt. The purpose of this provision is to provide help for people who do not own their own homes. It allows them to apply $400, plus any unused amount under paragraph (1), to protect other property—whether it is property which is exempt, but over the value permitted, or whether it is property which is normally not exempt, such as cash or money in a bank account.

In some cases, you may be better off selecting the exemptions permitted by state law. It is not possible in the space of this chapter to list the exemptions available in every state. Before you file for bankruptcy, you should try to find out about the state exemptions by checking with the clerk of the bankruptcy court. The clerk may be able to give you a list of the state exemptions or refer you to the state law which contains the exemptions.

If you are filing a joint petition with your spouse, each person may claim a separate list of exemptions. Sometimes it is possible to take advantage of both the federal and the state exemptions. The law provides that one of you may use the state list and the other the federal list.

Summary of Debts and Property. This form merely summarizes the information in the Statement of All Debts and the Statement of All Property.

List of Creditors. As soon as you file your petition for bankruptcy, the court will notify all of your creditors of the action you have taken and give them an opportunity to respond. To assist in this notification procedure, you must list on the List of Creditors the names and addresses of all the people and organizations to whom you owe money. This list should correspond to the information you included on your Statement of All Debts.

Application to Pay Filing Fees in Installments. It is not surprising that some people who file for bankruptcy are in such dire straits that they cannot afford to pay the $60 filing fee. If so, they can apply to pay the fee over time.

Filing the Forms

Your bankruptcy forms should be typewritten if at all possible. If not, then you should print clearly in ink. If you have any difficulty filling out or understanding the forms, ask for the assistance of the clerk of the bankruptcy court. The clerk is not permitted to give you legal advice, but one of his functions is to see that the forms are filled out and filed properly. You must file four copies of each form with the clerk's office. If, after you have filed, you remember another debt, or another asset, you can amend the forms—although there will be an additional $10 charge.

Bankruptcy court is part of the federal court system. When you file your bankruptcy petition, you must do so in the bankruptcy court in the federal district in which you live. They are usually located in major cities. Your check or money order must be made payable to the proper district, so make certain that you have the correct information before filing.

You do not have to file your papers in person. You can mail them, if you wish. The filing of these forms in bankruptcy court is known as an Order for Relief.

The Bankruptcy Procedure

As soon as your forms are received by the clerk of the bankruptcy court, the bankruptcy procedure begins. The court will advise all your creditors (according to your List of Creditors) of the action you have taken, and from that time on your creditors may not put pressure on you to pay what you owe. If one of these creditors does attempt to collect from you, simply advise him of your bankruptcy petition and the bankruptcy number assigned to you by the court.

Once you have filed a bankruptcy petition, you will be notified of the date of your first court appearance, which is known as "the first meeting of creditors." This meeting usually takes place within 40 days of the date of your filing, although it can be postponed if you have a good reason, such as illness. At this meeting, your creditors will have an opportunity to question you about your assets and debts and to obtain information about your financial condition. Some of your creditors may decide not to show up at the meeting, especially if they have reason to believe that they will not be able to recover any money in the bankruptcy proceeding.

In the past, the first meeting of creditors was presided over by the bankruptcy judge. But this has changed under the new law, and now the judge may not preside over or attend the meeting.

Usually, a "trustee" will be appointed by the court prior to the first meeting of creditors. The role of the trustee is to collect the property of the debtor and administer that property during the bankruptcy proceedings. The trustee also serves as a representative of the creditors, although in some cases this may require him to take action against certain creditors who have received or seek to receive benefits to which they are not entitled. In most cases, the trustee will be an attorney in private practice. However, the new bankruptcy law provides that in some districts there will be a special "United States Trustee" appointed by the Attorney General.

Probably most of the questions asked at the first meeting of creditors will come from the trustee. Under the provisions of the bankruptcy law, you are required to cooperate with the trustee and provide him with all of the books, documents, and records relating to your property.

The trustee may ask you whether you made any payments to creditors in the months prior to your filing for bankruptcy. The trustee can go back through your payments to determine if any such payments were made. Under the law, the trustee can void any payment made to a creditor on the basis of a prior debt if the payment was made within 90 days of the date of filing. He can then require that the payments be returned and added to your general assets for a more equitable distribution among your cred-

itors. If you transferred any assets or property to an "insider"—
that is, a relative or business partner—the trustee can void the
transfer if it occurred within 90 days of the date of filing. If you
transferred assets or property to an "insider" between 90 days and
one year before the date of filing, the trustee can void the transfer, but only if he can show that the insider who received the
property had "reasonable cause" to believe that you were insolvent.

After the meeting of creditors, it is up to the bankruptcy judge
to determine, according to certain well-established principles and
guidelines, how your debts will be discharged.

First of all, there are certain debts and obligations which *cannot* be discharged. These include the following important items:

1. All tax claims which became due within three years preceding bankruptcy. (The debtor cannot obtain a discharge of a
   tax liability—no matter how old—if he failed to submit a
   tax return or made a false or fraudulent statement on the
   return).
2. Alimony, maintenance, or support payments to a spouse or
   child.
3. The claims of creditors which you failed to list in your bankruptcy petition.
4. An educational loan owed to a governmental unit or non-
   profit institution of higher education unless the loan became
   due five years before the date of filing of your petition or
   unless the court determines that payment of the loan would
   impose an undue hardship on you or your dependents.
5. Any debt obtained on the basis of fraud or the filing a false
   financial statement which was reasonably relied on by the
   creditor.

This last item may be important if you have any outstanding
loans or credit obligations. Suppose that prior to filing for bankruptcy, you obtained a loan from the Easy Money Finance Company. To obtain this loan, you were required to fill out an
extensive questionnaire, listing all of your assets and liabilities.
Unfortunately, when you completed the form, you failed to include some of the debts owed to banks and credit-card companies. The Easy Money Finance Company may make an
appearance in bankruptcy court and claim that the amount still
owed on the loan should not be discharged because you filed a
false financial statement.

When the bankruptcy judge has made a determination with

respect to your case, he will schedule a hearing, which you must attend. At the hearing, the judge will announce which of your debts have been discharged. If any particular debt has not been discharged, the judge must explain to you the reason why it has not been discharged. If you have decided to "reaffirm" or pay on the debts owed to a creditor, the judge must inform you of the legal effects and consequences of reaffirming the debt.

Fraud

In these proceedings, the bankruptcy judge will, of course, consider all of the information in your petition, as well as any report or recommendation made by the trustee. Your debts will not be discharged by the judge if he finds that you have engaged in fraudulent conduct.

In one case, a Florida resident received substantial amounts in the form of disability payments and civil-service commissions, which he deposited in the bank. He then decided to take off on an extended trip through Europe for "relaxation." During the trip, he incurred over $25,000 in debts to American Express, Master Charge, BankAmericard, and a Greek department store. While these debts continued to pile up, he permitted his disability-insurance stipends and civil-service monies to accumulate in segregated savings accounts, and made no attempt to use these funds to offset even day-to-day expenses for necessities. The debtor then filed a petition for voluntary bankruptcy, listing as creditors all the credit-card companies and firms whose bills remained unpaid. The debtor claimed that these companies could not reach the funds in his savings accounts since this money came from disability payments and civil-service commissions— which were exempt under the law. The bankruptcy judge decided that the debtor had engaged in "a premeditated and deliberate plan" to defraud his creditors and ruled that his debts should not be discharged.

In most bankruptcy proceedings, the debtor is protected because most of his property is exempt and cannot be reached by creditors. But what happens if he has extra cash on hand? Some experts in bankruptcy law believe that a debtor should take most of his extra cash and "invest" the money in exempt assets before filing for bankruptcy. Others claim that a debtor who does this is engaged in unethical and fraudulent conduct.

In one court case, a debtor in Oregon stated that he purchased a rifle just before bankruptcy in order to enjoy the exemption accorded by Oregon for a rifle. The judge refused to allow him to take the exemption, claiming that he purchased the rifle with "a fraudulent intent." Most courts, though, would probably take a more lenient approach and allow the debtor to take the exemption.

This particular issue was raised in Congress when the new bankruptcy law was debated. The individuals who helped draft the law were asked whether a debtor could shift assets to take advantage of the allotted exemptions. They submitted a report which stated, "As under current law, the debtor will be permitted to convert non-exempt property into exempt property before filing a bankruptcy petition. . . . The practice is not fraudulent as to creditors, and permits the debtor to make full use of the exemptions to which he is entitled under the law."

Special Problems

If you are planning to file a petition for bankruptcy, you are probably concerned about what effect this will have on your everyday affairs. Will you still be able to obtain all of the essential services that you need? Will the gas and electric companies shut off service if you owe them money and you file a petition in bankruptcy court?

Under the new law, a utility may not discontinue service because you have filed a bankruptcy petition. However, you or the trustee appointed in your case must provide the utility with adequate assurance of payment for future service in the form of a deposit or security within 20 days of the date that your petition is filed—or the utility may halt service. The bankruptcy judge does have the power to reduce the amount of deposit or security requested by the utility.

The next thing you must consider is what happens to your automobile. If you purchased the automobile by obtaining a loan from a bank, you may have signed an agreement giving the bank a security interest in the automobile. If you still owe money on the loan at the time that you file for bankruptcy, the bank will be considered a "secured creditor." This means that the bank has the right to repossess the automobile. If you need the car to drive to work or for any other purpose, you may want to make special arrangements with representatives of the bank so that you can keep the car and continue to make payments. Or you may want to "redeem" the automobile under a special provision of the new bankruptcy law.

The provision concerning your right to redeem property is a bit confusing, so it is best to try to explain it by way of example. Suppose that you own a $2,000 car and you still owe the bank $1,200 in payments. Your interest in the car is $800. This $800 interest is exempt, since under the law you can claim an exemption in an automobile up to $1,200. You can redeem the automobile by paying the bank the $1,200 owed. Then you will be able to keep the car free and clear of all claims by the bank.

What type of property can be redeemed? Any personal property which is intended primarily for personal, family, or household use.

How do you redeem property under the law? The new rules provide that the trustee appointed in your case must ask the court to hold a hearing. After the hearing, the court may authorize you to redeem the property.

Suppose that you borrow money from a small loan company and sign a loan agreement giving the company a security interest in all of your household goods. If you file for bankruptcy, can the loan company seize all of your furniture and other possessions? Under the new bankruptcy law, the loan company cannot seize this property if it is exempt under the law and falls within the following categories:

1. Household furnishings, household goods, wearing apparel, appliances, books, musical instruments, or jewelry.
2. Professional books or tools of a trade.
3. Professionally prescribed health aids.

Some individuals who file for bankruptcy are uncertain about what to do with money they receive after the date of filing. Remember that your creditors are only entitled to share in the assets and property held by you on the date of filing. Any money that you receive after this date is usually not considered part of the bankruptcy estate. There are some exceptions to this rule including (1), tax refunds and (2), money received from an inheritance or as a result of a property settlement with your spouse within six months of the date of filing your petition. If you receive a paycheck from your employer for work performed after you filed the petition, it cannot be claimed by your creditors. To make things easier for you, you should deposit any "new money" received after the date of filing in a separate checking or savings account. In this way, you can maintain a clear distinction between the assets subject to the bankruptcy court and the money which you can use to pay future bills.

If the bankruptcy judge does decide to discharge all of your debts at the final hearing, you will be given a clean slate. But you will have to be more careful about how you handle your finances. Once your debts have been discharged in bankruptcy court, you cannot file for bankruptcy again for another six years.

Repayment Plan

Until now, we have been discussing "straight bankruptcy," which is a procedure for obtaining the prompt discharge of most debts. Another possibility worth considering is the filing of an individual debt-repayment plan. This is an arrangement that stops short of straight bankruptcy, but that nevertheless provides for an orderly recovery from a difficult financial situation. Here, briefly, is how it works.

A person who is deeply in debt and is finding it impossible to make payments to creditors when they come due works out a plan for the repayment of those debts over a longer period of time, usually up to thirty-six months. The debtor submits this plan to the bankruptcy court, and after the court "confirms" the plan, the debtor makes the regular agreed-upon payments. In the meantime, the debtor is given the same protection from creditor harassment as he would have had under straight bankruptcy.

Before the court will confirm the debtor's repayment plan, however, the debtor must show that the plan is workable. To do so, the debtor works out a budget, showing all income and all normal monthly expenses. The debtor also lists all debts, distinguishing between those that are secured and those that are unsecured. Secured creditors usually receive all or a substantial part of the money owed. The trustee in the case receives a fee or commission of five percent of all payments made under the plan.

The amount of money paid to creditors must be within the debtor's ability to pay as indicated by the debtor's budget. For example, if the debtor decides to pay creditors a total amount of $7,200 and the plan calls for repayment in thirty-six months at $200 a month, the debtor's budget must show that his income exceeds his regular monthly expenses by at least that amount. If the size of the monthly payments exceeds the debtor's ability to pay, the court will not confirm the plan.

The procedure for filing such a debt-repayment plan is similar to that for filing a bankruptcy petition. The repayment-plan forms are usually available at stationery stores. After these forms are filled out they must be filed with the clerk of the bankruptcy court, at which time creditors are automatically prevented from harassing the debtor for payment.

As with bankruptcy, the debtor must submit to the court a list of the names and addresses of all creditors. The court will then notify those creditors of the action taken and advise them of the date set for a meeting—called a confirmation hearing—of all creditors who wish to ask questions or raise objections to the plan.

Confirmation of the debtor's plan does not require approval and agreement on the part of unsecured creditors, but it does require that such creditors receive at least as much as they would receive if the debtor chose to file for straight bankruptcy. This is almost certain to be the case because very often unsecured creditors receive nothing in a straight bankruptcy proceeding.

Secured creditors are placed in a better position. Before a plan is confirmed they must either (1), consent to the plan (2), obtain the right to repossess or recover the secured property, or (3), retain a lien on the property and receive money or property that is not less than the amount of the secured claim.

Once the debtor has completed payments under the plan, the court will grant a discharge of all the debts included in the plan.

UNITED STATES BANKRUPTCY COURT FOR THE   SOUTHERN   DISTRICT OF   NEW YORK

*In re

JOHN SMITH

CASE NO.

_____ Debtor

CHAPTER 7

Include here all names used by debtor within last 6 years.

(If this form is used for joint petitioners wherever the word "petitioner" or words referring to petitioners are used they shall be read as if in the plural.)

VOLUNTARY CASE: DEBTOR'S *JOINT* PETITION[1]

1. Petitioner's post-office address is   802 East 23rd Street, Apt. 13L
                                         New York, New York 10010

2. Petitioner has

    ☒ resided within this district for the preceding 180 days.

    ☐ had his*(her)* domicile within this district for the preceding 180 days.

    ☐ had his*(her)* principal place of business within this district for the preceding 180 days.

    ☐ resided or been domiciled or had his*(her)* principal place of business within this district for a longer portion of the preceding 180 days than in any other district.

3. Petitioner is qualified to file this petition and is entitled to the benefits of title 11, United States Code as a voluntary debtor.

Wherefore, petitioner prays for relief in accordance with chapter 7 of title 11, United States Code.

Signed: ....

[148]

Petitioner

Petitioner

Address........802 East 23rd Street, Apt. 13L

......New York, New York 10010

DECLARATION[2]

INDIVIDUAL: I,   John Smith   the petitioner named in the foregoing petition, certify under penalty of perjury that the foregoing is true and correct.

JOINT INDIVIDUALS: We,   and   the petitioners named in the foregoing petition, certify under penalty of perjury that the foregoing is true and correct.

CORPORATION: I,   the   of the corporation named as petitioner in the foregoing petition, certify under penalty of perjury that the foregoing is true and correct, and that the filing of this petition on behalf of the corporation has been authorized.

PARTNERSHIP: I,   a member — an authorized agent — of the partnership named as petitioner in the foregoing petition, certify under penalty of perjury that the foregoing is true and correct, and that the filing of this petition on behalf of the partnership has been authorized.

Executed on   19   Signature:...............

Petitioner

....

Petitioner

© 1979 JULIUS BLUMBERG, INC.

Form Nos. 1 & 2 combined & 5, chapter 7, Voluntary case : debtor's petition individual, joint, corporation and partnership, 10-79.

1 The filing of a joint petition is authorized by 11 U.S.C. §302.
2 The unsworn declaration conforms with Public Law 94-550, 90 Stat. 2534, 28 U.S.C. §1746 (1976) which permits the declaration to be made in the form indicated with the same force and effect as a sworn statement.
3069   Form Nos. 1, 2 & 5, chapter 7.

© 1979 JULIUS BLUMBERG, INC.

In re

JOHN SMITH

} CASE NO.

Debtor

Include here all named used by debtor within last 6 years.

(If this form is used by joint debtors wherever the word "debtor" or words referring to debtor are used they shall be read as if in the plural).

Schedule A — STATEMENT OF ALL LIABILITIES OF DEBTOR

Schedules A-1, A-2, and A-3 must include all the claims against the debtor(s) or debtors' property as of the date of the filing of the petition by or against debtor.

SCHEDULE A-1 — CREDITORS HAVING PRIORITY

(1) Nature of Claim	(2) Name of creditor and complete mailing address including zip code (if unknown, so state)	(3) Specify when claim was incurred and the consideration therefor; when claim is contingent, unliquidated, disputed, or subject to setoff, evidenced by a judgment, negotiable instrument, or other writing, or incurred as partner or joint contractor, so indicate; specify name of any partner or joint contractor on any debt.	(4) Indicate if claim is contingent, unliquidated or disputed.	(5) Amount of Claim
a. Wages, salary, and commissions, including vacation, severance and sick leave pay owing to workmen, servants, clerks, or traveling or city salesmen on salary or commission basis, whole or part time, whether or not selling exclusively for the debtor, not exceeding $2,000 to each, earned within 90 days before filing of petition or cessation of business, if earlier (specify date).	None			$
b. Contributions to employee benefit plans for services rendered within 180 days before filing of petition or cessation of...	None			

None

None
None
None

c. Deposits by individuals, not exceeding $100 for each for purchase, lease, or rental of property or services for personal, family, or household use that were not delivered or provided.

d. Taxes owing (itemize by type of tax and taxing authority:)

(1) To the United States

(2) To any State

(3) To any other taxing authority

Total   0

Form No. 6, Schedule A-1, 10-79

3072   Form No. 6, page 1

[151]

Schedule A-2 — Creditors Holding Security

(1) Name of creditor and complete mailing address including zip code (if unknown, so state)	(2) Description of security and date when obtained by creditor	(3) Specify when claim was incurred and the consideration therefor; when claim is contingent, unliquidated, disputed, subject to setoff, evidenced by a judgment, negotiable instrument, or other writing, or incurred as partner or joint contractor, so indicate; specify name of any partner or joint contractor on any debt.	(4) Indicate if claim is contingent, unliquidated or disputed	(5) Market value	(6) Amount of claim without deduction of value of security
City Finance, 987 Broadway, New York, NY 10010 Security in household possessions, Loan renewed in 7/79. Undisputed				$ 1800.00	$ 4320.00
			Total	$ 1800.00	$ 4320.00

[152]

Schedule A-3 — Creditors Having Unsecured Claims Without Priority

Name of creditor (including last known holder of any negotiable instrument) complete mailing address including zip code (if unknown, so state).	Specify when claim was incurred and the consideration therefor; when claim is contingent, unliquidated, disputed, subject to setoff, evidenced by a judgment, negotiable instrument, or other writing, or incurred as partner or joint contractor, so indicate; specify name of any partner or joint contractor on any debt.	Amount of Claim
Unicharge P.O. Box 1001 New York, NY 10017	Revolving charge account, plus accrued interest. Undisputed	$ 1,157 89
Credicard P.O. Box 1980 Phoenix, AZ 85001	Revolving charge account, plus accrued interest. Undisputed	899 53
Elite Department Store 198 E. 57th Street New York, NY 10022	Revolving charge account, plus accrued interest. Undisputed	999 36
Investor's Book Club P.O. Box 1234 Montclair, NJ 07044	Books, 10/79 Undisputed	78 24
Paul Smith 13808 Lafayette Blvd. Jamaica, Queens, NY 11415	Personal Loan, 7/79 Undisputed	5,000 00
ABC Department Store 1700 Lexington Avenue New York, New York	Revolving charge account, plus accrued interest. Undisputed	1,040 00
	Total	$ 9,175 07

Form No. 6, Schedule A-2 & A-3, 10-79

3072   Form Nos 6, page 2

[153]

SCHEDULE B — STATEMENT OF ALL PROPERTY OF DEBTOR

Schedules B-1, B-2, B-3, and B-4 must include all property of the debtor as of the date of the filing of the petition by or against debtor.

Schedule B-1 — Real Property

Description and location of all real property in which debtor has an interest (including equitable and future interests, interests in estates by the entirety, community property, life estates, leaseholds, and rights and powers exercisable for the benefit of debtor)	Nature of interest (specify all deeds and written instruments relating thereto)	Market value of debtor's interest without deduction for secured claims listed in schedule A-2 or exemptions claimed in schedule B-4
None		$
		Total 0

Type of Property	Description and location	Market value of debtor's interest without deduction for secured claims listed on schedule A-2 or exemptions claimed in schedule B-4
a. Cash on hand		$
b. Deposits of money with banking institutions, savings and loan associations, credit unions, public utility companies, landlords, and others	(1) Checking account: Citibank, 14th & Irving New York, NY 10003 (2) Rent deposit: Building Management, Inc. 804 E. 14th St., New York, NY 10003	78 53 290 00
c. Household goods, supplies, and furnishings	2 sofas, eight chairs, television, table, bed, 4 lamps, chest of drawers, refrigerator	1,800 00
d. Books, pictures, and other art objects; stamp, coin, and other collections	Books	100 00
e. Wearing apparel, jewelry, firearms, sports equipment, and other personal possessions	Wearing apparel, watch	500 00
f. Automobiles, trucks, trailers, and other vehicles	1976 Ford Mustang	1,500 00
g. Boats, motors, and their accessories	None	
	Total	

Form No. 6. Schedule B-1 & B-2. 10-79

3072   Form No. 6. page 5

[155]

Schedule B-2 — Personal Property (Continued)

	Type of property	Description and location	Market value of debtor's interest without deduction for secured claims listed on schedule A-2 or exemptions claimed in schedule B-4
h.	Livestock, poultry, and other animals	None	$
i.	Farming supplies and implements	None	
j.	Office equipment, furnishings, and supplies	IBM Electric Typewriter	350 00
k.	Machinery, fixtures, equipment, and supplies (other than those listed in items j and l) used in business	None	
l.	Inventory	None	
m.	Tangible personal property of any other description	None	
n.	Patents, copyrights, franchises, and other general intangibles (specify all documents and writings relating thereto)	None	
o.	Government and corporate bonds and other negotiable and nonnegotiable instruments	None	

p. Other liquidated debts owing debtor   None

q. Contingent and unliquidated claims of every nature, including counterclaims of the debtor (give estimated value of each)   None

r. Interests in insurance policies (itemize surrender or refund values of each)   None

s. Annuities   None

t. Stocks and interests in incorporated and unincorporated companies (itemize separately)   None

u. Interests in partnerships   None

v. Equitable and future interests, life estates, and rights or powers exercisable for the benefit of the debtor (other than those listed in schedule B-1) [specify all written instruments relating thereto]   None

Total $4,618 53

[157]

Form No. 6 Schedule B-2 (Continued), 10-79

3072   Form No. 6, page 6

Schedule B-3 — Property Not Otherwise Scheduled

Type of property	Description and location	Market value of debtor's interest without deduction for secured claims listed in schedule A-2 or exemptions claimed in schedule B-4
a. Property transferred under assignment for benefit of creditors, within 120 days prior to filing of petition (specify date of assignment, name and address of assignee, amount realized therefrom by the assignee, and disposition of proceeds so far as known to debtor)	None	$
b. Property of any kind not otherwise scheduled	None	

[158]

Total

Form No. 6, Schedule B-3 & B-4, 10-79

Debtor selects the following property as exempt pursuant to [X] 11 U.S.C. §522(d) [ ] the laws of the State of ....

Schedule B-4 — Property Claimed as Exempt

Type of property	Location, description, and so far as relevant to the claim of exemption, present use of property	Specify statute creating the exemption	Value claimed exempt
2 sofas ($200 each)	Residence of debtor	522 (d) (3)	$ 400 00
8 chairs ($50 each)	Residence of debtor	522 (d) (3)	400 00
television	Residence of debtor	522 (d) (3)	200 00
table	Residence of debtor	522 (d) (3)	200 00
twin bed	Residence of debtor	522 (d) (3)	200 00
4 lamps ($25 each)	Residence of debtor	522 (d) (3)	100 00
chest	Residence of debtor	522 (d) (3)	100 00
refrigerator	Residence of debtor	522 (d) (3)	200 00
books	Residence of debtor	522 (d) (3)	100 00
watch	Residence of debtor	522 (d) (4)	500 00
Elec. typewriter	Residence of debtor	522 (d) (5)	350 00
Ford Mustang	Residence of debtor	522 (d) (2) and (5)	1,500 00
checking account	Citibank	522 (d) (5)	78 53
Rent deposit	Building Management, Inc.	522 (d) (5)	290 00
		Total	4,618 53

[159]

3072   Form No. 6, page 7

SUMMARY OF DEBTS AND PROPERTY

(From the statements of the debtor in Schedule A and B)

Schedule		Total

DEBTS

Schedule		Total
A—1/a, b.	Wages, etc. having priority	—
A—1(c)	Deposits of money	—
A—1/(d) 1.	Taxes owing United States	—
A—1/(d) 2.	Taxes owing states	—
A—1/(d) 3.	Taxes owing other taxing authorities	—
A—2	Secured claims	$4,320.00
A—3	Unsecured claims without priority	$9,175.07
	Schedule A total	$13,495.07

PROPERTY

Schedule		Total
B—1	Real property (total value)	—
B—2/a.	Cash on hand	—
B—2/b.	Deposits	368.53
B—2/c.	Household goods	1,800.00
B—2/d.	Books, pictures, and collections	100.00
B—2/e.	Wearing apparel and personal possessions	500.00
B—2 f.	Automobiles and other vehicles	1,500.00
B—2/g.	Boats, motors, and accessories	—
B—2/h.	Livestock and other animals	—
B—2/i.	Farming supplies and implements	—
B—2/j.	Office equipment and supplies	350.00
B—2/k.	Machinery, equipment, and supplies used in business	—
B—2/l.	Inventory	—
B—2/m.	Other tangible personal property	—
B—2/n.	Patents and other general intangibles	—
B—2/o.	Bonds and other instruments	—
B—2 p.	Other liquidated debts	—
B—2 q.	Contingent and unliquidated claims	—
B—2/r.	Interests in insurance policies	—
B—2/s.	Annuities	—

B—2/t .... Interests in corporations and unincorporated companies. .... —

B—2/u .... Interests in partnerships. .... —

B—2/v .... Equitable and future interests, rights, and powers in personalty. .... —

B—3/a .... Property assigned for benefit of creditors. .... —

B—3/b .... Property not otherwise scheduled .... —

Schedule B total $ 4,618.53

UNSWORN DECLARATION UNDER PENALTY OF PERJURY

INDIVIDUAL(S): I(*we*)   John Smith   *and*   sheets, and that they are true and
certify under penalty of perjury that I(*we*) have read the foregoing schedules, consisting of
correct to the best of my(*our*) knowledge, information, and belief.

CORPORATION: I,   the (*insert president or other officer or an authorized agent*)
of the corporation named as debtor in this case, certify under penalty
of perjury that I have read the foregoing schedules, consisting of   sheets, and that they are true and correct to the best of my
knowledge, information, and belief.

PARTNERSHIP: I,   a (*insert member or an authorized agent*)
of the partnership named as debtor in this case, certify under penalty
of perjury that I have read the foregoing schedules, consisting of   sheets, and that they are true and correct to the best of my
knowledge, information, and belief.

Executed on   19

....
Signature

....
Signature

[161]

United States Bankruptcy Court for the SOUTHERN District of NEW YORK

In re

JOHN SMITH

                    Debtor

CASE NO.

STATEMENT OF
FINANCIAL AFFAIRS FOR DEBTOR
NOT ENGAGED IN BUSINESS

Include here all names used by debtor within last 6 years.

Each question should be answered or the failure to answer explained. If the answer is "none," this should be stated. If additional space is needed for the answer to any question, a separate sheet, properly identified, and made a part hereof, should be used and attached.

The term "original petition," as used in the following questions, shall mean the petition filed under Rule 1002, 1003, or 1004.

(If this form is used by joint debtors wherever the word "debtor" or words referring to debtor are used they shall be read as if in the plural.)

1. **Name and residence.**

  a. What is your full name and social security number?   John Smith 024 68 9753

  b. Have you used, or been known by, any other names within the 6 years immediately preceding the filing of the original petition herein?   No
(If so, give particulars.)

  c. Where do you now reside?   802 East 23rd Street, New York, NY

  d. Where else have you resided during the 6 years immediately preceding the filing of the original petition herein?

2. **Occupation and income.**

  a. What is your occupation?   Computer Programmer

  b. Where are you now employed?   Data Systems, 3456 Ave. of Americas (6 years)
(Give the name and address of your employer, or the address at which you carry on your trade or profession, and the length of time you have been so employed or engaged.)

  c. Have you been in a partnership with anyone, or engaged in any business during the 6 years immediately preceding the filing of the original petition herein?   No
(If so, give particulars, including names, dates, and places.)

  d. What amount of income have you received from your trade or profession during each of the 2 calendar years immediately preceding the filing of the original petition herein? $18,000 per annum from July, 1979 to present
$16,000 per annum prior to July, 1979

  e. What amount of income have you received from other sources during each of these 2 years?   None
(Give particulars, including each source, and the amount received therefrom.)

3. **Tax returns and refunds.**

  a. Where did you file your federal and state income tax returns for the 2 years immediately preceding the filing of the original petition herein?   (a) Federal: Holtsville, N.Y.
State: Albany, N.Y.

  b. What tax refunds (income and other) have you received during the year immediately preceding the filing of the original petition herein?   (b) $344.40 Federal
35.25 State
26.20 City

  c. To what extent tax refunds (income or other), if any, are you, or may you be, entitled?

[162]

4. Bank accounts and safe deposit boxes.

a. What bank accounts have you maintained alone or together with any other person, and in your own or any other name within the 2 years immediately preceding the filing of the original petition herein?
(Give the name and address of each bank, the name in which the deposit is maintained, and the name and address of every other person authorized to make withdrawals from such account.)

b. What safe deposit box or boxes or other depository or depositories have you kept or used for your securities, cash, or other valuables within the 2 years immediately preceding the filing of the original petition herein?
(Give the name and address of the bank or other depository, the name in which each box or other depository was kept, the name and address of every other person who had the right of access thereto, a brief description of the contents thereof, and, if the box has been surrendered, state when surrendered, or, if transferred, when transferred, and the name and address of the transferee.)

Citibank, 14th & Irving Pl., New York, N.Y. in the name of John Smith

None

5. Books and records.

a. Have you kept books of account or records relating to your affairs within the 2 years immediately preceding the filing of the original petition herein?

b. In whose possession are these books or records?
(Give names and addresses.)

c. If any of these books or records are not available, explain.

d. Have any books of account or records relating to your affairs been destroyed, lost or otherwise disposed of within the 2 years immediately preceding the filing of the original petition herein?
(If so, give particulars, including date of destruction, loss, or disposition, and reason therefor.)

Check stubs in debtor's possession

Bank statements discarded when reconciled with own records. Four most recent statements retained.

6. Property held for another person.

What property do you hold for any other person?
(Give name and address of each person, and describe the property, or value thereof, and all writings relating thereto.)

None

7. Prior bankruptcy.

What proceedings under the Bankruptcy Act or title 11, United States Code have previously been brought by or against you?
(State the location of the bankruptcy court, the nature and number of each case, the date when it was filed, and whether a discharge was granted or refused, the case was dismissed, or a composition, arrangement, or plan was confirmed.)

None

[163]

8. Receiverships, general assignments, and other modes of liquidation.

a. Was any of your property, at the time of the filing of the original petition herein, in the hands of a receiver, trustee, or other liquidating agent?

(If so, give a brief description of the property, the name and address of the receiver, trustee, or other agent, and, if the agent was appointed in a court proceeding, the name and location of the court, the title and number of the case, and the nature of the proceeding.)

No

b. Have you made any assignment of your property for the benefit of your creditors, or any general settlement with your creditors, within one year immediately preceding the filing of the original petition herein?

(If so, give dates, the name and address of the assignee, and a brief statement of the terms of assignment or settlement.)

No

9. Property in hands of third person.

Is any other person holding anything of value in which you have an interest?

(Give name and address, location and description of the property, and circumstances of the holding.)

No

10. Suits, executions, and attachments.

a. Were you a party to any suit pending at the time of the filing of the original petition herein?

(If so, give the name and location of the court and the title and nature of the proceeding.)

No

b. Were you a party to any suit terminated within the year immediately preceding the filing of the original petition herein?

(If so, give the name and location of the court, the title and number of the case, and nature of the proceeding, and the result.)

No

c. Has any of your property been attached, garnished, or seized under any legal or equitable process within the year immediately preceding the filing of the original petition herein?

(If so, describe the property seized or person garnished, and at whose suit.)

No

11. Loans repaid.

What repayments on loans in whole or in part have you made during the year immediately preceding the filing of the original petition herein?

(Give the name and address of the lender, the amount of the loan and when received, the amounts and dates of payments and, if the lender is a relative or insider, the relationship.)

Monthly payments of $68.00 to Citibank, 14th and Irving Place, New York, NY. Auto loan, 8/78. Monthly payments of $88.00 to City Finance, 987 B'way, New York, NY. Loan renewed, 9/79. (see annexed page for details)

12. Transfers of property.

a. Have you made any gifts, other than ordinary and usual presents to family members and charitable donations, during the year immediately preceding the filing of the original petition herein?

(If so, give names and addresses of donees and dates, description, and value of gifts.)

No

b. Have you made any other transfer, absolute or for the purpose of security, or any other disposition, of real or tangible personal property during the year immediately preceding the filing of the original petition herein?

No

[164]

13. Repossessions and returns.

Has any property been returned to, or repossessed by, the seller or by a secured party during the year immediately preceding the filing of the original petition herein?
(If so, give particulars including the name and address of the party getting the property and its description and value.)

No

14. Losses.

a. Have you suffered any losses from fire, theft, or gambling during the year immediately preceding or since the filing of the original petition herein?
(If so, give particulars, including dates, names, and places, and the amounts of money or value and general description of property lost.)

b. Was the loss covered in whole or part by insurance?
(If so, give particulars.)

No

15. Payments or transfers to attorneys.

a. Have you consulted an attorney during the year immediately preceding or since the filing of the original petition herein?
(Give dates name and address.)

Yes. Aug., 1979. Charles Brady, 148 Fifth Ave., New York, N.Y.

b. Have you during the year immediately preceding or since the filing of the original petition herein paid any money or transferred any property to the attorney or to any other person on his behalf?
(If so, give particulars, including amount paid or value of property transferred and date of payment or transfer.)

Yes. $300.00 to Charles Brady for divorce in Aug. 1979.

c. Have you, either during the year immediately preceding or since the filing of the original petition herein, agreed to pay any money or transfer any property to an attorney at law, or to any other person on his behalf?
(If so, give particulars, including amount and terms of obligation.)

Only above payment.

UNSWORN DECLARATION UNDER PENALTY OF PERJURY

I (We), _____ John Smith _____ and _____

certify under penalty of perjury that I (we) have read the foregoing schedules, consisting of _____ sheets, and that they are true and correct to the best of my (our) knowledge, information, and belief.

Executed on _____ 19___

_____
Signature

_____
Signature

© 1979 JULIUS BLUMBERG, INC.

© 1979 JULIUS BLUMBERG, INC.

Small Claims Court

Almost everyone has purchased household furniture or had an automobile or television set repaired, usually without any complications. Occasionally, however, problems develop. The furniture, for example, may be delivered in damaged condition, or the charges for the automobile repair may far exceed the original estimate.

Suppose something like that happened to you. And suppose the people at the store or the garage were completely unresponsive to your complaints. What recourse would you have? You might hire a lawyer, but the legal fees may exceed the amount of money involved in the dispute. Another possibility would be to take the matter to Small Claims Court.

What Is Small Claims Court?

Small Claims Courts are special courts established by a number of cities and states to enable persons to resolve disputes involving limited amounts of money without becoming entangled in complicated and costly legal proceedings.

Thousands of years ago, when two people had a dispute, they would bring the matter to the head of the family or clan. The two parties would each present their side, and the leader would make a decision. Today, however, our system of justice is considerably more elaborate. The complexities of the law have increased to such an extent that the texts on the rules of evidence alone fill several bookcases in a law library. A complicated antitrust case, for example, can take ten years to wend its way through the legal system, and the legal fees for the parties involved can amount to hundreds of thousands of dollars. Yet this same system must find a way to resolve a dispute over $50 between a consumer and a merchant. It is generally recognized that Small Claims Court is the best way to resolve such conflicts.

Although procedures vary depending on the city or town where you live, the atmosphere is generally informal, and arbitrators, rather than judges, are sometimes used to decide the cases. Some courts even schedule sessions in the evening so consumers can have their cases heard without having to be away from their jobs. Also, you can usually file suit and obtain a hearing in a matter of weeks. And best of all, you don't have to hire a lawyer to present your case, which is why Small Claims Court is frequently referred to as "People's Court." (There is a list at the end of this chapter which provides basic information about Small Claims Court procedures in forty major cities.)

What Kinds of Cases Are Heard in Small Claims Court?

Most of the cases heard in Small Claims Court involve "breach of contract"—that is, one party claims that another party has failed to abide by an agreement. Here are a few examples of cases that can be heard in Small Claims Court:

1. A claim that a laundry or dry cleaner lost or damaged clothing.
2. A claim that a repairman charged too much or failed to repair an item properly.
3. A claim by a tenant that a landlord refused to return a security deposit.
4. A claim that someone damaged a car and refused to pay for repairs.
5. A claim that a travel agent failed to arrange a tour as promised.
6. A claim that a store delivered shoddy merchandise.

Some cases are obviously not suited for Small Claims Court. If you feel that someone has made untruthful statements about you and you want to sue for libel or slander, you should not take your case to Small Claims Court. If someone has taken your idea or has copied a story or article you have written, you should not try to resolve the dispute in Small Claims Court. If you have suffered serious physical or emotional injury as a result of an accident, you should consult with an attorney rather than press the case in Small Claims Court. If you have been discriminated against because of your race, religion, or sex, you should not attempt to obtain restitution in Small Claims Court. Because these cases involve amounts in excess of Small Claims Court limits, they should be heard on more advanced levels of the state or federal court system.

Who Can Sue in Small Claims Court?

Any person can bring an action in Small Claims Court. A minor may sue by having a parent or guardian file the case. In some places, a corporation or partnership may not file suit in Small Claims Court because authorities do not want business entities to use the court as a mill to collect consumer debts.

There is no requirement that a lawyer file the case or represent you at the hearing. In fact, hearing officers and arbitrators often bend over backward to help the layperson. You can hire a lawyer if you wish, but in a small case the legal fees can equal or exceed the amount in issue in the case.

What Can You Sue For in Small Claims Court?

There is a limit, which varies from place to place, on the amount of money that can be sought in Small Claims Court. In New York City the maximum is $1,000. In Los Angeles the maximum is $750. (For other cities, see the list at the end of the chapter.)

What should you do if you have a claim for $600, but the limit in your area is $500? You can sue for $500 and forego the additional $100. Or you can sue in a "higher" court for the $600. You cannot bring a second action in Small Claims Court to collect the additional $100.

A person suing in Small Claims Court requests a judgment for *compensatory damages*—that is, an amount of money which will compensate him for damages actually sustained. If you purchase a vacuum cleaner for $80 and the vacuum cleaner does not work, you can sue to recover the $80. Or if the vacuum cleaner can be repaired, you can sue to recover the cost of repairs. In either case, you can also request court costs and interest.

You cannot, however, collect for "aggravation." For example, if a dry cleaner ruined the clothes you had planned to wear to your friend's wedding, you can sue the dry cleaner to recover the value of the clothes, but you cannot recover an additional amount for the annoyance that he caused you.

As a general rule, Small Claims Court can only grant monetary damages. The court does not provide *equitable relief*, which means that the court will not issue an injunction preventing another party from acting. You cannot bring an action in Small Claims Court, for example, to prevent your neighbor from playing his stereo late at night.

The purpose of Small Claims Court is to provide substantial justice for the parties involved, according to the circumstances of each particular case, as illustrated by the following decision by a judge in New York City's Small Claims Court:

"The question presented by this interesting small claims case is whether a woman who buys a membership in a health club may get her money back when the health club is transformed into a massage parlor.

"Plaintiff holds a responsible position with one of the television networks. In January, 1971, when her physician advised her to take up swimming, she went looking for a health club. It was easy to find one. Defendant's health club was located in the very building where plaintiff lived. It had a swimming pool, a gymnasium, and separate saunas and showers for men and for women. Plaintiff joined.

"Her membership ran to January, 1972. All went well, and, on January 28, 1972, plaintiff signed a contract renewing her membership for another year. The fee was $220, which she paid.

"Almost immediately, plaintiff became ill. She could not use the club's facilities for about six weeks. Defendants were sympathetic, and agreed, in substance, that plaintiff's contract would be deemed to run from March 15, 1972, to March 15, 1973.

"Plaintiff used her new membership in late March or early April. She entered the women's sauna. A nude man was in it. She retreated to the women's shower, where she found another nude man washing himself. She retreated again and sought the owner, who was nowhere to be found. Plaintiff never returned.

"In October, the club was raided. The police arrested 14 young women and 2 male employees on prostitution charges. But since the complaints were dismissed in Criminal Court, the raid plays no part in my decision. What does is defendants' advertising leaflet, printed on pink paper, embellished with a photograph *une grande horizontale*, and captioned, 'There's a new sport in town.' The text runs as follows: 'Now you can sneak away at lunch or right after work to New York's most unique and beautiful key club. Experience the ultimate in total relaxation. A trained team of lovely masseuses are waiting to rub your weary body back to life in one of our many private massage rooms. Massage is just one of the many services available to you at no extra charge. . . . Apply now. A limited number of charter keys are still available. Open 12:00 noon 'til 2:30 A.M. Major credit cards accepted.'

"So much for the facts. Now for law. The contract reflects a bargain between plaintiff and defendants whereby plaintiff paid $220 and defendants were to make available to plaintiff for a period of one year the facilities of the health club. Implicit in defendants' promise was the further promise that a health club it would be: not a bordello, not a dance hall, and not, as it became, a massage parlor. When defendants changed the nature of the enterprise, they breached their implied promise to plaintiff. Since the breach was substantial, plaintiff in turn had the right to rescind. I find that plaintiff exercised this right with reasonable promptness, and so conclude that 'substantial justice between the parties . . .' requires a judgment for $220 in plaintiff's favor".

A novel claim of breach of contract involved a San Jose man who sued a San Francisco woman for breaking a date. The plaintiff, according to a newspaper report, claimed the woman broke an "oral contract" to have dinner and see a show with him. The plaintiff wanted to be paid for two hours spent driving to and from San Francisco at his minimum rate as a CPA of $8.50 an hour and 17 cents a mile for auto expenses. The total claim was for $34, plus filing fees.

The woman who was sued said she thought the plaintiff was

"nuts" to think she would pay. The judge apparently agreed: "The promise to engage in a social relationship for one evening in exchange for affection and/or one evening at the theater is unenforceable under the law of contracts."

How Do You Start the Suit?

To sue someone in Small Claims Court, you, as plaintiff, must go to the office of the clerk of the court to file a complaint against the other party, who becomes the defendant. It is best to call in advance to determine when the clerk's office is open, the amount of the filing fee (usually about $5), and the procedure for serving the complaint, or summons, on the defendant. (Most Small Claims Courts will serve the papers on the defendant for a small fee.) You must also be sure that you are taking your case to the Small Claims Court—which is only a local or neighborhood court—that has *jurisdiction* over the defendant. This is not a problem if you and the defendant live in the same city or town. But if the defendant lives in another city, you may have to file your complaint there.

When you file the complaint, the clerk will ask you for the name and address of the person you are suing. You must be able to give the clerk the exact legal name. If you are suing an individual, you must supply the full name. You cannot sue "Willie the Snake" even if everyone in the neighborhood knows who he is. If you are suing a business, you must have the full legal name of that business. First check the sales slip or contract to see if the company name is printed at the top. If not, call the company and ask for the correct legal name. Finally, you can contact the office of the county clerk to find out whether the legal name is on file there. (The sales slip may say Smith Importers, but the corporate records at the county clerk's office may show that the proper name is Smith Importers, Inc.)

This information is extremely important. If you do not know the correct legal name of the party you wish to sue, you may not be able to recover your money.

New York State has recently passed a new law making it easier for consumers to collect Small Claims Court judgments against business entities. Under the old law, consumers could not collect if the judgments were not in the official corporate name of the business. Under the new law, judgments may contain the "everyday name" of the business, as it appears in a telephone directory or on a storefront window.

You can sue more than one person in Small Claims Court. If you have a legitimate doubt which of two parties is responsible, sue both and let the court decide which one is liable.

When you go to the clerk's office, you will be asked to explain the nature of the suit. It is best to prepare for this question in advance, so you can provide a succinct answer. Example: "I purchased a sofa for $700, but it was delivered with the wrong color fabric. I want to sue to recover the purchase price." Bring all receipts, documents and letters to the clerk's office so you can answer any questions. Before you leave the clerk's office, you should ask for: (1) the index number of the case, (2) the date scheduled for trial, and (3) the time when you should be in court.

Should You Settle the Case Out of Court?

After you file your complaint, the defendant, or the defendant's lawyer, may call you to discuss a settlement. A settlement usually involves an agreement to pay some, but not all, of the money demanded in a suit. A cynic once remarked that a fair settlement is one that satisfies neither of the parties.

It is impossible to make hard and fast rules about the settlement of a case. Generally, if you can obtain 75% of the amount you have requested, it would be considered a good settlement. This varies, of course, with the circumstances. If you have paid $600 for a new sofa, and the merchant has failed to deliver, you may not want to accept a settlement offer of only $450. But if you have taken a two-year-old coat to the dry cleaner and he has burned a hole in the sleeve, you should be willing to settle for a figure below 75%. If the case goes to trial, the court will undoubtedly consider the fact that the coat is two years old in determining the amount of damages to be awarded. You may have to accept an amount which represents 20% or 25% of the purchase price of the coat.

There are some general principles to follow in discussing settlement with the other side. You should try to get the defendant to make a definite offer; otherwise you may be bidding against yourself. Assume that you have filed suit for $300, and the defendant starts the discussion by asking you to name a more reasonable figure. If you say $200, the defendant may say that this is still too high and break off the negotiations. In this case nothing is accomplished, since the defendant has not made an offer and you have already reduced your demand by $100. Do not concede too quickly. Once you have placed a figure on the table, you cannot realistically expect the defendant to settle for a greater amount.

If the defendant is represented by a lawyer, you may actually have an advantage in negotiating a settlement. The defendant will have to pay the attorney $50 or $100 just to appear in court. Thus it would be advantageous for the defendant to work out a settlement before the day of trial, otherwise the attorney's legal fees will have to be paid along with any judgment that may be awarded by the court.

If the defendant agrees to settle the case, try to collect before the date of the trial. If this is not possible, be sure to contact the clerk of the court to find out how to adjourn, or postpone, the case pending receipt of the money from the defendant. If you simply let the trial date pass without taking any action, and if later you are unsuccessful in collecting the money agreed upon in your settlement agreement, it will be much more difficult and much more complicated to begin the procedure all over again.

Sometimes the parties can agree on a settlement that does not involve the payment of money. If you have purchased a defective TV or other merchandise, the store may agree to replace the item for you. In this case you should put the settlement agreement in writing and make certain that a store official signs the agreement, promising to replace the item by a fixed date. Again, if you cannot obtain complete satisfaction before the trial date, be sure you obtain an adjournment.

After settlement has been reached, the other side may ask you to sign a *release*. A release is a statement discharging the other side from all claims or actions which exist at that time. The release is usually set forth on a printed legal form supplied by the defendant or the defendant's lawyer. The release should be transmitted at the same time that the money is paid. If the defendant is represented by an attorney, you may be asked to send the release to the attorney's office before the check is forwarded to you. If you send the release, write a covering letter stating that the release has been sent with the understanding that the attorney will hold it *in escrow* until you have received the check—and it has cleared.

Preparing for Trial

If the case is not settled, there are some basic steps you should take to prepare for trial. First, collect all of the contracts, receipts, bills, and letters which are relevant to the case. You should review all of these papers so that you have a clear idea of the events that occurred.

Next you should make an outline of the case, noting all significant dates and events. If you are suing to obtain a refund from a store, your outline may look like this:

> March 3: Went to Smith Department Store, fifth floor, purchased sofa for $695. Salesman said it would be delivered in brown suede. Paid $200 deposit. Received sales receipt, which says: "Sofa, brown suede."
>
> March 21: Called store to confirm delivery date. Store clerk said sofa would be delivered on April 10.
>
> April 10: Store delivered sofa with solid-blue fabric. I refused to sign for merchandise and delivery men reloaded the sofa. Called store and spoke to Mr. Marshall, supervisor of the Home Furnishings Department. He promised to check on the problem and call me back.
>
> April 15, 17, 18: Called the store, but personnel refused to discuss the problem. On April 18, Mr. Marshall finally told me that the brown suede sofa was no longer in stock.
>
> April 20: Wrote letter to Smith Department Store demanding refund of $200 deposit. No answer was ever received.

You should review the outline several times before you appear in court. It is not advisable to write a prepared statement or memorize a speech for the court. It is sufficient to have recall of the major facts of the case.

If there are witnesses who can support your claim, you should notify them of the date and time of trial. If the witness is reluctant to appear, you should serve a *subpoena*, which is a legal document requiring a person to appear in court. Since the procedures for issuing a subpoena are not the same in every jurisdiction, you should ask the clerk of the court how this is done. You do not have to serve a subpoena on the defendant, since the defendant, as a party to the case, must appear in court.

While you are waiting for the trial date, you may be notified that the defendant has filed a *counterclaim*. A counterclaim is a claim made by the defendant against the plaintiff, usually involving the same dispute. In the example above, Smith Co. may allege that it performed all of the terms and conditions of the contract and submit a counterclaim for $400, the balance of the purchase price under the contract. If a counterclaim is filed against you, the court will hear your claim and the counterclaim at the same time. However, if the defendant submits a counterclaim for more than the jurisdictional limit, say $1,500, the court may remove the entire case to a higher court. Often a counterclaim is filed for tactical reasons, hoping that, with a counterclaim pending, the plaintiff will be more willing to negotiate a settlement.

A special note should be made at this point about adjournments. If you or one of your witnesses is unable to come to Court, you should request an adjournment, in which case you may be required to submit a letter or affidavit. Check with the clerk's office to find out the procedure for your case.

The Trial

Many people have a distorted picture of what happens during a trial. Their impressions have been formed by watching television shows about lawyers, particularly the old Perry Mason classics. A real trial rarely has the same suspense as a television drama. It is unlikely that any case you will see in Small Claims Court will end with the defendant on the witness stand sobbing, "I did it. I did it."

There is very little in the way of excitement or drama in a Small Claims Court proceeding. The judge or arbitrator will simply listen to both sides and try to render a decision that will result in substantial justice for both parties.

On the day set for trial, remember to take with you all contracts, receipts, bills, and documents relating to the case. (It is surprising how many people forget to bring these papers.) It is also important to appear in court on time. In most places, the clerk begins the session by reading the *calendar*, which is the docket or list of cases to be heard that day. If you are not present when the calendar is read, the clerk may dismiss your case.

In some courts the clerk also gives instructions to the parties. These instructions could include the room where the cases will be heard or the order in which they will be called. In some cities the clerk also asks the parties to decide whether they wish to have the case heard by a judge or by an arbitrator. In New York City the clerk reads the following statement in court:

"It would be physically impossible for the one judge sitting here tonight to try all cases on the calendar; therefore, at the request of the court we have several arbitrators who possess the qualifi-cations of a judge of this court to hear this case. You obtain an immediate trial if you go before the arbitrators. The only differ-ence is that you will not be able to appeal from the arbitration award. When your name is called, you will be sent out to an arbitrator unless you state that you wish the judge to hear your case."

It is important, therefore, to listen to all of the instructions and to pay attention when the calendar is read. When the case is called by the clerk, the defendant may request an adjournment. If an adjournment is granted and a new date set, be certain that you make a record of that date.

If the defendant fails to appear, an *inquest* may be held instead of a trial. At an inquest, you must show that you are entitled to recover damages, and it should be much easier for you to do so since the defendant will not be there to contradict your state-ments.

If both parties are present, the case will be marked ready and brought before a judge or arbitrator. Normally, the judge or ar-bitrator will ask the parties to give a brief explanation of the case. In some instances, the judge or arbitrator may make a suggestion concerning settlement. If the parties cannot agree on a settle-ment, the trial will begin.

The plaintiff (or the party who files suit) is the first to give testimony. The clerk reads the oath—"Do you swear to tell the truth, the whole truth, and nothing but the truth, so help you God?"—and then the plaintiff is asked to give an account of the dispute.

If you are the plaintiff, you should explain to the court exactly what happened, supplying names and dates when appropriate. Take as much time as you need. Remember that Small Claims Court is the "People's Court." No one expects you to perform like a seasoned trial lawyer.

If there are any contracts, documents, or letters which support your claim, you should show them to the judge or arbitrator. If you purchased defective merchandise, you may wish to exhibit the merchandise in court to prove your point. At times, the judge may interrupt you to ask a question. Try to respond to each question asked as completely as possible, even if it seems to involve a minor point.

When you have completed your testimony, the defendant or the defendant's lawyer may cross-examine you. In cross-examination, the other side tries to bring out points which are favorable to its side of the case. Respond to each question with a short, simple statement. Don't try to outguess the other side or try to figure out why a particular question was asked.

Next, the court hears testimony from any witness you wish to call. These witnesses may also be cross-examined by the other side.

The defendant is then permitted to present the other side of the case. Most likely the defendant will try to explain why you have no right to the relief requested. Do not interrupt, even when a clear misstatement of fact is made. When the defendant is finished, you will then be given an opportunity to cross-examine, at which time you can challenge any misstatements by asking questions or by showing bills, receipts, or other documents which contradict the defendant's testimony. If you feel that the defendant has concentrated on irrelevant or unimportant points, try to get the court to focus on the main issues.

At the trial, you must establish a *prima facie* case, which means that you must prove all of the essential elements of your case, including the amount of damages. It is usually said, therefore, that the burden of proof is on the plaintiff. Once you have met this burden, the defendant must come forward to rebut your claims. The court will decide in your favor if you have proved your case by a preponderance of the credible evidence.

The decision of the court is usually mailed to the parties a short time after the trial. In some cities the decision is rendered the same evening. If you are a successful plaintiff, the decision may appear in the following form:

This action having duly come on for trial before me on May 15, 1979, an after-trial judgment is awarded in favor of the plaintiff in the amount of $200, plus interest, and court costs in the amount of $3.20.

R. Jones
City Judge

Collecting the Judgment

Winning a judgment in Small Claims Court is only half the battle. The party who wins must also try to collect the money from the other side. Unfortunately, a large number of judgments are never collected. The percentage of uncollected judgments may reach 50% or 60% in some cities. With this in mind, there are some steps you can take to collect a money judgment awarded by the court.

First, you should communicate with the defendant or the defendant's lawyer and request payment. If you have obtained a judgment against a department store or major company, the chances are excellent that you will be paid. (Of course, if the company files an appeal, the judgment will be stayed, or delayed, pending determination of the appeal.) However, a defendant who has limited funds or is annoyed at losing the case may refuse to pay the judgment.

If this happens, you should contact the office of the clerk of the court. The clerk will probably direct you to the sheriff or marshal who is authorized to execute the judgment against the defendant's property, which means that certain of the defendant's property can be seized and sold to satisfy the judgment. Or a certain percentage of the defendant's salary can be seized and turned over to you until the judgment is paid.

You can also compel the defendant to come into court and be examined under oath in order to obtain information about bank accounts and other assets. In some jurisdictions, it is possible to obtain a restraining order which ties up money in the defendant's bank account. Again, the clerk of the court can guide you on the proper procedure to follow in your area.

If the defendant owns a house, you may file a transcript of the judgment with the county clerk (or the appropriate local official) where the house is located. This will prevent the defendant from selling or otherwise disposing of the house without first satisfying the judgment.

Remember that you collect only from the defendant named in the court papers. If you filed suit against Smith Importers, Inc., you can execute on property owned by Smith Importers, Inc., but you cannot seize funds held in the personal bank account of John Smith, president of the corporation.

If the defendant is licensed by a state or city agency, you may be able to exert additional leverage. Some businesses which are frequently licensed are employment agencies, dry cleaners, TV repair shops, auto mechanics, vocational schools, and home-improvement contractors. On the basis of your complaint, the government agency may try to persuade the licensee to pay the judgment. If the agency is aggressive in protecting consumer rights, it may threaten to revoke or suspend the license until all small claims judgments are paid.

Court administrators are now placing more emphasis on helping people to collect judgments obtained in Small Claims Court. New York City makes available consumer counsel and attorneys to provide information about collecting judgments. New York has also passed a law which provides that triple damages may be assessed against a defendant who has failed to pay three small claims judgments. You should be able to determine, with a little investigation, where similar help is available in your area.

SMALL CLAIMS COURTS

LOCATION	HOURS	LIMIT	FEES
Akron 837 City Court Safety Bldg. (216) 375-2922	M,T,Th,F —3:45 p.m. W —7:00 p.m. Sa —9:00 a.m.	$500	$7.50
Atlanta 103 State Court Bldg. 160 Pryor St., S.W. (404) 572-2101	1st & 4th Tu each month —9:30 a.m.	$299.99	$8–$14
Baltimore Fayette & Gay Sts. (301) 383-4520	M,T,W,Th,F —9:15 a.m. & 1:30 p.m.	$500	$5—filing $2.50—service by mail $5—service by constable
Birmingham Court House, Room 516 (205) 325-5331	M,T,W,Th,F —8:00 a.m.	$500	$10.50
Boston Boston Municipal Court Pemberton Square (617) 725-8413, 8414	M,T,W —2:00 p.m.	$750	$4.40
Buffalo 50 Delaware Ave. (716) 847-8290	W —2:00 p.m. 3rd W 7:00 p.m.	$1,000	$2—filing $1.40—service
Chicago Pro Se Court Room 2600, Daley Center (312) 443-8155	M,T,W,Th,F —9:30 a.m.	$500	$12—filing $11 + 30¢ a mi.— service

Location	Days	Hours	Bond	Fees
Cincinnati Alms & Doepke Bldg. 222 E. Central Pkwy. (513) 632-8891	M,W,F	—1:00 p.m.	$500	$6—filing $2.50—service
Cleveland 2nd Level, Justice Center 1200 Ontario St. (216) 664-4860	M,T,W,Th,F	—1:30 p.m.	$500	$6
Columbus 375 S. High St., 16th Floor (614) 222-7381	T,W,Th	—1:30 p.m.	$500	$10
Dallas New Courthouse, Ground Floor (214) 749-8591	M,T,W,Th,F	—9:00 a.m.	$200–$500	$7—filing $4—service
Dayton 367 W. Second St. (513) 225-5363	Tu	—9:00 a.m. & 1:30 p.m.	$500	$10—filing $6—service
Denver City & County Bldg., Room 31	M,T,W,Th,F W (once monthly)	—1:30 p.m. & 3:00 p.m. —6:00 p.m.	$500	$9
Detroit City-County Bldg., Room 1101 1 Woodward (313) 224-5467	M,T,W,Th,F	—8:30 a.m. & 2:00 p.m.	$300	$7—filing $6—service
Fort Worth Civil Courts Bldg. (817) 334-1438	M,T,W,Th,F	—8:00 a.m.	$150–$500	$8-15
Houston Through local justices of the peace	M,T,W,Th,F		$150–$200	$7

SMALL CLAIMS COURTS (continued)

LOCATION	HOURS		LIMIT	FEES
Indianapolis				
Center Division				
City County Bldg., Room G-5	Tu	—9:00 a.m.	$1,500	$20
(317) 633-3657				
Decatur Division				
3059 Kentucky Ave.	Tu	—9:00 a.m.	$1,500	$20
Lawrence Division				
4611 Franklin Rd.	Tu	—9:00 a.m.	$1,500	$20
Perry Division				
5552 Madison Ave.	Tu	—9:00 a.m.	$1,500	$20
Pike Division				
5450 Lafayette Rd.	Tu	—9:00 a.m.	$1,500	$20
Warren Division				
5924 E. 10th St.	Tu	—9:00 a.m.	$1,500	$20
Washington Division				
2070 E. 54th St, Room 12	Tu	—9:00 a.m.	$1,500	$20
Wayne Division				
2424 W. 16th St.	Tu	—9:00 a.m.	$1,500	$20
Kansas City	M,T,W,Th,F	—8:30 a.m.	$500	$5–10
415 E. 12th St.				
Jackson Co. Court House				
(816) 881-3162				
Los Angeles	Daily	—9:00 a.m. &	$750	$2—filing
110 N. Grand Avenue, Room 429		1:00 p.m.		$3—service by mail
(213) 974-6133				$8—service by marshal

Location	Days / Hours	Amount	Fees
Louisville Hall of Justice 600 Jefferson St. (502) 588-4475	M,T,W,Th,F —9:00 a.m. M,T,W, —1:30 p.m.	$500	$13.58—filing $3—service (plus mileage)
Miami Dade County Courthouse, Room 138 73 West Flagler St. (305) 579-3726	M,T,W,Th,F —8:00 a.m.	$2,500	$6-20—filing $4.40—service by mail $12—service by sheriff
Milwaukee 901 N. Ninth St. (414) 278-4121	M,T,W,Th,F —9:00 a.m.	$1,000	$7—filing $5—service
Minneapolis 857-C Government Center (612) 348-2602	Daily —9:15 a.m. & 2:00 p.m.	$1,000	$2
Newark 470 High St., Rcom 106 (201) 961-7204	Daily —9:00 a.m.	$500	$2.70, plus mileage
New Orleans Civil Court Bldg., Room 201 421 Loyola Avenue (504) 586-1232	M,T,W,Th,F —9:00 a.m.	$300	$15—filing $4—service by constable
New York City *Bronx County* (Bronx) 850 Walton Ave., Room 111 (212) 590-3569	M,T,W —6:30 p.m.	$1,000	$3.40
Kings County (Brooklyn) 141 Livingston St., Room 206 (212) 643-8180	M,T,W,Th —6:30 p.m.	$1,000	$3.40

SMALL CLAIMS COURTS (continued)

LOCATION	HOURS	LIMIT	FEES
New York City (Lower Manhattan) 111 Centre St. (212) 374-8402	M,T,W,Th —6:30 p.m.	$1,000	$3.40
New York County (Harlem) 170 E. 121st St. (212) 369-8811	Th —6:30 p.m.	$1,000	$3.40
Queens County (Queens) 120-55 Queens Blvd. (212) 520-3633	M,T,W,Th —6:30 p.m.	$1,000	$3.40
Richmond County (Staten Island) 927 Castleton Ave. (212) 442-8000	W —6:30 p.m.	$1,000	$3.40
Philadelphia Filbert & Juniper Sts., Room 43 12th Floor, City Hall Annex (215) MU 6-7987, 7988, 7989	M,T,W,Th,F —3:45 p.m.	$1,000	$11
Phoenix Various local justices of the peace (602) 262-8594, 8538	M, T,W,Th,F —8:00 a.m.	$999.99	$5—filing to $500 $10—filing over $500
Pittsburgh Courthouse 504 5th and Grand (412) 355-5622	M,T,W,Th,F —8:30 a.m.	$10,000	$15.50—filing $25-35—service by sheriff
Portland Multnomah County Courthouse 1021 SW 4th Ave., Room 106 (503) 248-3023, 3024	M,Th —9:00 a.m.	$500	$6.60—filing to $100 $10.80—filing over $100 $10—service
Rochester Hall of Justice, Room 1 (716) 428-6733	W 2nd W	9:30 a.m. & 1:30 p.m. 7:00 p.m.	$1,000	$5.60

Location	Days/Hours	Amount	Fees
Sacramento 720 9th St. (916) 440-5713	M,T,W,Th,F —8:00 a.m. Th —6:00 p.m.	$750	$2—filing $3—service by mail $8.50—service by marshal
St. Louis Civil Courts Bldg. 12th and Market Sts. (314) 622-4434	T,Th —1:30 p.m.	$500	$5–10—filing $6—service by sheriff $2.50—service by certified mail
San Antonio Various local justices of the peace (512) 220-2651	M,T,W,Th,F —8:00 a.m.	$150	$8
San Diego County Courthouse, Room 2005 (714) 236-2534	M,T,W,Th —8:15 a.m.	$750	$2—filing $3—service by mail $8.50—service by marshal
San Francisco City Hall, Room 164 (415) 558-3211	M,T,W,Th,F —8:15 a.m.	$750	$2—filing
San Jose 200 West Hedding (408) 299-2271	M,T,W,Th —8:00 a.m. & 1:00 p.m.	$750	$2—filing $3—service by mail
Seattle Twelve local District Courts (206) 344-4250	M,T,W,Th,F —8:30 a.m.	$500	$1
Toledo 555 N. Erie St. (419) 247-6362	M,W,Th,F —2:00 p.m.	$500	$6.50—filing $2.50—service by mail
Washington, DC 500 Indiana Ave. NW, Room JM-260 (202) 727-1760	M,T,W,Th, F,S —9:00 a.m. W —6:00 p.m.	$750	$1—filing $1—service by marshal $1.40—service by mail

Copyrights and Trademarks

The first article of the U.S. Constitution grants to Congress the power to "promote the progress of science and useful arts, by securing for limited times to authors and inventors the exclusive right to their respective writings and discoveries."

The exclusive rights granted to inventors are called patents; those granted to authors are called copyrights. The legal work connected with the securing of patents is so complex and specialized that only those lawyers who pass a qualifying examination are permitted to represent inventors before the Patent Office. Consequently, if you have an invention for which you would like to obtain a patent, we suggest that you contact a patent attorney. There are also special patent or invention development firms which often advertise in newspapers. These firms, for an upfront fee and an interest in any financial returns from your invention, claim that they will obtain patent protection for your invention and locate and represent you in dealings with someone who is in a position to exploit your invention. We suggest you be most careful in dealing with these firms. While some of these firms may be legitimate, some have been criticized by state attorneys-general and the Federal Trade Commission for unfair practices. The general procedure for obtaining a patent is described in the pamphlet "General Information Concerning Patents," which is available from the Superintendent of Documents, United States Government Printing Office, Washington, D.C. 20102.

Copyrights

Copyrights are a much simpler matter than patents and can be handled quite easily without a lawyer. You can obtain the application forms and detailed instructions by writing to the Copyright Office, Library of Congress, Washington, D.C. 20559.

After years of deliberation, Congress recently revised the Copyright Law. The summary that follows is based on that new law, which went into effect on January 1, 1978.

What Can Be Copyrighted?

According to the Copyright Law, copyrightable material falls into seven categories:
1. Literary works.
2. Musical works, including any accompanying words.
3. Dramatic works, including any accompanying music.
4. Pantomimes and choreographic works.
5. Pictorial, graphic, and sculptural works.
6. Motion pictures and other audiovisual works.
7. Sound recordings.

What you have created must make use of some tangible means of expression—such as the printed page, film, or sound recordings—that the rest of us can perceive. You cannot copyright an idea. For example, you cannot copyright a diet and thereby prevent people from using it unless they pay you a fee. Nor can you prevent someone else from expressing himself on the principles upon which your diet is based, so long as he does not copy your expressions. But you can write a book about your diet, copyright the book, and then collect a royalty for each copy sold if a publisher decides to publish it.

Exclusive Rights

The owner of a copyright has the exclusive right to make and distribute copies of the copyrighted work, to perform or display the work in public (in the case of musical, dramatic, and choreographic works, for example), and to create other works based on it.

There are limitations to such exclusivity, however. One such limitation says that the "fair use" of copyrighted materials for such purposes as criticism, news reporting, scholarship, or research is not an infringement of the copyright. Whether any such use is "fair" depends upon how, why, and what quantity of the material is used, and how its use affects the potential market or the value of the copyrighted work. The reproduction of substantial portions of a copyrighted work for the purposes of making a profit, thereby reducing the value of the work to the copyright holder, will certainly be considered an infringement of the owner's copyright.

Copyright Registration

A copyright comes into existence as soon as a work is created —that is, as soon as it is fixed in a tangible medium for the first time. This means that as soon as your novel comes out of your typewriter, or as soon as your musical composition is put on paper, you have a copyright in the work. (If the work was made while you were in someone else's employ and at the instruction of the employer, the copyright is held by the employer, unless the parties have expressly agreed otherwise in a signed written agreement.) It is important, however, that you register your claim to copyright with the Copyright Office in order to protect your work in the event of some future copyright infringement. You cannot sue an infringer unless you have registered your claim to copyright.

You can register your claim to copyright as soon as your work is created, although claims to copyright are usually registered at the time of publication. When your work is published, it is absolutely necessary that such publication include the required copyright notice, or else it may be considered to be in the public domain and anyone who wishes to do so will be free to reproduce it. The required notice consists of the symbol © (or the word "Copyright"), followed by the year of the first publication of the work and the name of the copyright owner. In the case of a sound recording, the symbol used is ℗, followed by the first date of publication and the name of the copyright holder. (The year need not be included when a pictorial, graphic, or sculptural work is reproduced in or on greeting cards, postcards, stationery, jewelry, dolls, toys, or any useful articles.) The law specifies that such copyright notice is to be affixed to the copies "in such manner and location as to give reasonable notice of the claim of copyright." In the case of a printed publication, the notice is customarily placed on one of the first few pages on the publication. In the case of sound recordings, the notice should appear on the label or the container.

Nowadays authors will frequently submit their written works to a number of publishers at the same time. There is some question whether or not such multiple submissions constitute publication, and to be on the safe side, an author would be well advised to include with such submissions the notation "All rights reserved. Not previously published." An even safer procedure would be to include the regular copyright notice and then register the claim to copyright with the Copyright Office.

When writing to the Copyright Office be sure to indicate the precise nature of the work you have created (whether a book, record, film, or play script) so that you will be sent the appropriate application form. The application form includes detailed instructions on how to fill it out. When you submit your application, you must include a $10 registration fee, along with a single copy of your work if it is unpublished, and two copies of the work if it has been published.

When the Register of Copyrights has determined that the material you submitted is copyrightable, a certificate of registration will be issued under the seal of the Copyright Office. The certificate will contain the information in the application (your name, title of the work, etc.), together with the number and the effective date of the registration. All works created by individuals after

January 1, 1978, remain under copyright until fifty years after the author has died.

Transfer of Ownership

If you are not going to publish your work yourself, you will probably look for someone to publish it for you—a book publisher in the case of a book, a magazine or newspaper publisher in the case of an article. When you enter into such an arrangement, you are transferring to the publisher—in exchange for a monetary consideration—some or all of the rights that you hold as the owner of the copyright. It is important that you understand precisely what rights you are transferring and what rights you are retaining.

A publisher who wants to publish your novel will generally use its standard form of contract specifying the precise nature of your relationship. This will describe not only what the publisher is authorized by you to do in terms of the publication and distribution of your work, but also what royalties are to be paid to you in exchange for such authorization. The contract will also specify the division of income should your book result in other editions (paperback, illustrated), a motion picture, a TV series, or some other derivative work. Generally, when you place your novel with a publisher, the publisher will see that your work is properly registered with the Copyright Office in your name, and will also oversee, on your behalf, the sale of most subsidiary rights. Since book publishing can become quite complicated, and the financial arrangements can be involved, it would be to your advantage, if possible, to secure the services of a literary agent. The usual 10% agent's commission will be a reasonable price to pay in return for the agent's expertise and familiarity with the literary marketplace.

Magazine and newspaper publishers, on the other hand, seldom draw up a contract in connection with an article. This is because the transaction is much simpler. You generally authorize the publication to run your article one time (granting the publisher "first serial rights") in exchange for a fixed fee. It is important, nevertheless, to confirm with the publisher precisely what rights he is purchasing. If the publisher purchases "all rights," for example, you will not be able to use your work for any other purpose without the publisher's permission. Also, be certain to find out whether the publication in which your article will appear is routinely registered with the Copyright Office by the publisher. If not, and if you feel there is a possibility that someone at some future time will attempt to infringe your copyright, then you should register your copyright yourself. If the publication is routinely registered, and you feel the need for copyright protection, request that the page on which your article appears include your copyright notice.

Infringement and Remedies

If someone makes use of your work without your authorization (other than the "fair use" described earlier), you may bring a court action against such an infringer of your copyright, if your claim to copyright is registered before the action is commenced. Based on the facts of the case, the court may issue a temporary or final injunction to prevent the continued infringement of your copyright. If the injunction is temporary, pending a further examination of the case, the court may order that all copies under question be impounded until the case is finally decided. If the court decides in your favor, you will be entitled to recover actual damages suffered by you, as well as any additional profits made by the infringer, as a result of the infringement of your copyright. To determine the amount of such profits, you need establish only the infringer's gross revenues, and the infringer must then establish the amount of deductible expenses. Instead of seeking damages and profits, you may elect to recover statutory damages, which the court may fix between $250 and $10,000 per infringement, without regard to either your actual damages or the defendant's profits. In addition, whichever type of remedy you elect, the court may make the defendant pay your costs and attorney's fees. However, if you lose, the court could make you pay these amounts to the defendant.

Most of the cases involving copyright infringement are filled with technical details and would probably be of interest only to attorneys specializing in the field. But there is one x-rated case which should bring some of the principles of copyright protection into focus.

Several years ago Walt Disney Productions filed suit against some movie producers to prevent them from using a song called "The Mickey Mouse March" in a movie entitled *The Life and Times of the Happy Hooker*. Apparently the song had been originally used by Disney Productions in connection with *The Mickey Mouse Club*, a television series. Now the court was asked to decide whether use of the music in this movie constituted "fair use."

The judge noted that in the movie there is a segment where three male actors sing some words of the "Mickey Mouse March," and for a period of approximately four to five minutes, the "Mickey Mouse March" is played as background music while the female protagonist of the film appears to simultaneously gratify the sexual desires of the three male actors. During this time the cast is bare except that the male actors are wearing Mousketeer hats similar to those worn by the performers in the TV productions of the *The Mickey Mouse Club*. The judge explained that parody of a copyrighted article is permissible in some situations, but only where the parodist does not appropriate a greater amount of the original work than is necessary "to recall or conjure up the object of his satire." He ruled that the use of the song was more than a parody—it was a complete copy of the copyrighted material—and he enjoined the defendants from further use of the song.

TRADEMARKS

A trademark is any mark used by a manufacturer or merchant to identify and distinguish his goods from those manufactured or sold by others. A trademark can be a word ("Camel" for cigarettes), a name ("Johnny Walker" for Scotch), a symbol (the Del Monte shield), a device (the distinctive bottle shape used by Haig & Haig for its "Pinch" Scotch), or a combination (the word "Camel" plus the famous depiction of the camel in front of pyramids). Trademarks also serve to guarantee the quality of the goods bearing the mark and, through advertising, to create and maintain a demand for the product.

Trademarks should be registered with the Patent and Trademark Office, but that registration does not in itself create or establish any exclusive rights to a trademark. Rights to a trademark are acquired only through use, and the use must ordinarily continue if those rights are to be preserved. If a trademark owner's rights are infringed by someone else's use of the mark, prior registration with the Patent and Trademark Office will prove to be helpful in establishing the validity of the owner's claim to the right of exclusive use of the mark.

In order to be eligible for registration, a mark must be in use in interstate or foreign commerce. If its use is in connection with the sale or manufacture of goods, the mark must appear on the goods or their containers, or on the displays associated with the goods, or on the tags or labels attached to the goods. If its use is in connection with services, then it must be displayed in the sale or advertising of the service.

Note: Trademarks differ from trade names. Trade names (nouns) are used to identify businesses; trademarks (adjectives) are used to distinguish goods or services. Trade names are not subject to registration with the Patent and Trademark Office; it may be a requirement that a trade name be registered with some state or local agency.

Information regarding trademarks (but not legal advice) may be obtained from the United States Trademark Association in New York City.

Application for Registration

The application for registration must be filed in the name of the owner of the mark, and the owner may file the application directly and without the use of a lawyer. Application forms for corporations, individuals, and firms are available from the Patent and Trademark Office. Your request should be addressed to the Commissioner of Patents and Trademarks, Washington, D.C. 20231. The useful and informative booklet "General Information Concerning Trademarks" is available from the Superintendent of Documents, Government Printing Office, Washington, D.C. 20402.

Application for trademark registration consists of a written application, a drawing of the mark, five specimens of the trademark, and the fee.

Written Application. Applications to the Patent and Trademark Office must either make use of the printed form provided by the office or must, if you prepare your own form, follow the same style closely. The application must be in the English language. If you prepare your own form, it must be plainly written and only one side of the paper. The Patent and Trademark Office prefers that you use legal-size paper and that the application be typewritten, double-spaced, with a 1½-inch margin on the left-hand side and the top of the page. The application must include, among other things, a request for registration, the name and address of the applicant, the particular goods on which the mark is used, the official classification of the goods (there are more than forty classifications; the Patent and Trademark Office will provide a list of the categories), the date on which the mark was first used, and the manner in which the mark is used. The application must also state that the applicant, or the firm, corporation, or association being represented, is the owner of the mark, and that no other person or organization has a right to use the mark either in the identical form or a form that so resembles the mark as to deceive or cause confusion.

Drawing. The Patent and Trademark Office requires that the drawing of the mark adhere to certain exact standards having to do with the size and quality of the paper, the kind of ink, the format, the character of the lines, the code for the identification of color, etc. If the instructions are not followed precisely, the application may be rejected until the deficiency is corrected.

Specimens. The five trademark specimens submitted must be actually used tags, labels, etc. Again, the instructions for submitting specimens are precise and must be followed faithfully.

Fee. The standard fee for an application to register a trademark is $35, although there is a schedule of charges and fees for other services the Patent and Trademark Office may be called upon to perform in connection with your application—if, for example, corrections must be made on your drawings, etc. Payment must be made in cash, postal money order, or certified check. If you send cash, send it by registered mail. If you send a money order or certified check, make it payable to the Commissioner of Patents and Trademarks. A personal check will delay your application until your check clears your bank.

Examination of Applications

Applications are docketed and examined in the order in which they are received. If the mark is not entitled to registration for any reason (either because it is something which is not registrable or because there is an existing registration with which it is in conflict), the applicant is notified and advised of the reasons and of any formal requirements or objections. The applicant then has six months in which to respond. Failure to respond within this period results in abandonment of the application. If the applicant responds as required, then the application will be reexamined or reconsidered. A final rejection can be appealed to the Trademark Trial and Appeal Board.

If it appears that the applicant is entitled to have the mark registered, it will be published in the *Official Gazette* and will be subject to opposition. Interested parties have 30 days from publication in which to oppose a mark's registration. If there is no opposition, a certificate of registration will be issued. The entire process, from application date to receipt of a certificate of registration, usually takes well over a year and often takes much longer.

A registrant should give notice that a mark is registered by displaying with the mark as used the words "Registered in U.S. Patent and Trademark Office," or "Reg. U.S. Pat. & Tm. Off.," or ®. Use of such notice before the actual issuance of a certificate or registration for the mark is improper and may be the basis for refusal of registration.

Registrations remain in force for twenty years from the date of registration and may be renewed for periods of twenty years from the expiration date unless previously canceled or surrendered.

A digest of registered marks is maintained in the Search Room of Trademark Operations in Washington and is open to the public. This digest includes a set of the registered word marks arranged alphabetically and a set of registrations comprising symbols, birds, animals, etc., arranged according to the classification of the goods or services with which they are used. It is advisable to search this digest before adopting a trademark so as to avoid possible conflict with previously registered marks.

Trademarks versus Corporate Names

It is a serious mistake for a businessman to assume that because he has been able to incorporate under a particular name he is free to use that name. This is by no means the case. When a secretary of state approves a new corporate name, all he indicates is that there is no other corporation organized under the laws of the state with the same or a similar name. There may be a corporation with the same name already incorporated in another state, or there may be a business with an entirely different name which is already using a trademark which is identical or similar to the corporate name you have selected and your secretary of state has cleared. In either case, if the other corporation or business is in the same type of business as you or a closely related type of business, your use of the corporate name may subject you to liability. It is not a good defense in court that your name has been cleared by one secretary of state.

If you plan to make a substantial investment in promoting your name, it would be wise to have your name searched by an organization (such as Trade Mark Service Corporation in New York) which will check registrations in the Patent and Trademark Office, state trademark registrations (see below), and trade directory listings for similar names and trademarks. All that need be submitted to the searching organization is the distinguishing portion of your corporate name and a short statement of the types of goods and/or services in which your business will deal. The cost of having a search made and having it analyzed by a person knowledgeable in trademark matters should be modest when compared with the investment you plan to make in promotion and may ensure against your having to change your name at some time after you already have spent a significant amount on promotion or advertising. There are some search firms that deal only through lawyers, however, so you should check to make sure you can use the firm's services on your own.

State Trademark Registrations

All of the states have passed laws which enable you to register your trademark with the state's secretary of state. This process is different from having the secretary clear a corporate name. While a state trademark registration is not a substitute for a federal registration with the Patent and Trademark Office, it does have some advantages, primarily for the business which will be local in its scope.

A state registration is relatively simple, inexpensive ($10–50), and quick to obtain. Each secretary of state will provide a printed form on which your application may be filed, and instructions for doing so. The time between filing the application and receiving the Certificate of Registration is usually one month or less. The chief advantage of a state registration is that it prevents someone else from later registering a similar trademark in your state. Also, it creates a public record of the facts surrounding your use of the mark. If someone later is interested in using a similar trademark and has this mark searched by a searching organization, your registration will be found and may dissuade the latecomer from proceeding with his plans. Finally, if you have to sue someone for infringement, the state registration may be used as evidence of your rights.

Glossary

abandonment—the act of a husband or wife who leaves his or her spouse voluntarily and without just cause. Sometimes referred to as "desertion."

accessory—a person who aids or assists in the commission of a crime. An "accessory after the fact" is one who has knowledge that a crime has been committed and conceals it from the law or harbors or assists the person who committed the crime.

accomplice—a person who voluntarily joins with the principal offender in the commission of a crime.

acquit—to set free or release. A person who is found not guilty by a jury is "acquitted."

affidavit—a sworn statement submitted by a person with knowledge of the facts.

alibi—an explanation made by a person charged with a crime that, at the time the crime was committed, he was at another place. A defendant may allege that on the evening a murder was committed he was visiting his ailing mother.

alimony—financial support or maintenance for a spouse, usually after divorce. Some feminists now contend that the word "alimony" has an unsavory connotation, and they prefer to use the expression "spousal support."

annulment—a declaration by a court of law that a marriage is void from its inception. In the eyes of the law, the marriage never existed.

answer—a written response made by a person served with legal papers. If Joe sues Frank and serves him with a complaint, Frank must submit an answer within a proscribed period of time.

appeal—an application to a higher court to reverse or modify a decision or judgment made by a lower court.

appellant—the person who files an appeal.

arbitration—submission of a legal dispute to a person or panel for resolution. Although the arbitrator is not a judge, the decision is usually binding on all parties.

arraignment—proceeding in which a person charged with a crime is brought before the court and asked to plead guilty or not guilty to the charges. An arraignment takes place well before the trial.

attorney—an advocate or counsel who represents a person in court or renders legal advice or assistance. Also known as counselor-at-law, lawyer, and, in England, solicitor or barrister.

bail—an amount of money which must be paid or pledged before a person charged with a criminal offense is released pending trial. The amount of bail is usually set by a judge at the arraignment.

bailment—delivery of personal property to another to hold. A bailment can be gratuitous or it can be in exchange for a fee. When you take a suit to a dry cleaner, you are creating a bailment.

bankruptcy—a special proceeding involving a person or firm who is insolvent and unable to pay all outstanding debts. In general terms, the purpose of the proceeding is to permit the bankrupt to be discharged of all existing debts; any assets which exist, however, are usually divided among the creditors. A bankruptcy proceeding can be voluntary (initiated by the debtor) or involuntary (initiated by the creditors).

bequest—to give personal property to another by will. The words "bequest" and "devise" are often used synonymously.

bill of particulars—a written statement or explanation of the charges filed in a lawsuit. In practice, the party who is sued sometimes serves a demand for a bill of particulars on the party who filed the action. The response is called the bill of particulars.

Bill of Rights—the first Ten Amendments to the United States Constitution.

breach of contract—failure to perform one of the terms or provisions of a contract.

bylaws—the rules or regulations of a corporation. The bylaws usually provide for the election of the board of directors, the duties and responsibilities of corporate officers, etc.

calendar—the list of cases to be heard by a court of law. An attorney will usually "put a case on the calendar" for trial when all discovery has been completed.

chattel—an article of personal property, although in the broader sense it may include animate as well as inanimate objects.

civil action—a lawsuit brought to recover damages or obtain vindication of some right (as opposed to a criminal proceeding, in which one is charged with a violation of law by the state).

class action—a lawsuit filed on behalf of numerous other people. The court must issue a special order recognizing the suit as a class action. To maintain a class action in federal court, the person filing the suit must meet a number of tests and must show that (1) the class is composed of numerous persons, (2) there are questions of law and fact common to the class, (3) the claims made by the person filing suit are typical of the claims of the people in the class, and (4) the person filing suit will fairly and adequately protect the interests of the class.

codicil—an addition or supplement to a will signed by the testator.

common law—the body of law and jurisprudence which was originally developed in England and adapted to a great extent by the United States (as distinguished from the laws and statutes enacted by our legislative bodies).

complaint—the legal papers served by the person who starts a lawsuit. The complaint states the grounds for the suit and the relief requested from the court.

community property—in states which have community property laws, all of the property acquired during the marriage by either spouse. This property is, in effect, owned by both of them. States which have community property laws are: Arizona, California, Idaho, Louisiana, Nevada, New Mexico, Texas, and Washington.

condonation—forgiveness or acceptance of improper behavior or conduct by a spouse.

consideration—payment or value given to another person to induce him or her to enter into a contract.

Constitution—written instrument establishing the American form of government and providing for a separation of powers between the executive, legislative, and judicial branches. There are now twenty-six amendments to the Constitution.

contract—a promise or set of promises which the law will enforce. (See Chapter 1.)

copyright—the right of the author or creator to a literary or artistic work. The holder of a copyright has the exclusive right to make and distribute copies of the work. (See Chapter 11.)

co-signer—a person who signs a contract or loan agreement at the request of the buyer or borrower, usually to help him obtain credit. If the buyer or borrower fails to make payments, the creditor can sue the co-signer to collect the balance due.

counterclaim—a claim presented by a defendant in opposition to a lawsuit. If James sues Matthew for breach of contract, Matthew may include a counterclaim against James in his answer.

damages—the loss or injury suffered by a party. A person filing a lawsuit will usually request monetary damages to compensate him for the injury suffered. *Liquidated damages* refers to a specific amount of damages set in advance by the parties to a contract. For example, the parties may specify in the contract that "in the event of a breach of contract or default by either party, the amount of damages will be fixed at $2,000." Provisions fixing liquidated damages will be enforced only if they are reasonable.

de facto—in fact, or in deed. This phrase is often used to describe an action or procedure which is adopted or maintained even though it has no legal foundation. (Opposite of "de jure," which means rightful or legitimate.)

declaratory judgment—a judgment which declares the rights of the partics or establishes the opinion of the court on a question of law. A person may file suit asking the court to issue a declaratory judgment that a specific law or procedure is unconstitutional.

deed—a written instrument by which one person conveys land to another.

default—the omission or failure to perform as agreed.

default judgment—a judgment obtained when the party sued fails to appear or file papers. A default judgment may sometimes be "reopened" if it can be shown that the person sued had no notice of the suit. (See *sewer service*.)

deposition—testimony of a witness usually taken before trial (sometimes called an "EBT"). Also a statement made under oath.

devise—a gift of real property, usually by will.

discovery—process by which an attorney tries to obtain information prior to trial (includes interrogatories and depositions).

dismissal—an order or judgment ending a lawsuit. A "dismissal with prejudice" means that the case is ended and cannot be started again.

divorce—final dissolution of a marriage. "Limited divorce" usually refers to a divorce from "bed and board" or a "judicial separation." (See Chapter 6.)

domicile—place where a person lives. The legal definition is something more than mere "residence," since "domicile" assumes an intention to remain.

dower—the legal right of a widow to a portion of her husband's estate. (Not to be confused with "dowry.")

EBT—examination before trial; oral testimony given by a party or witness prior to the trial. The testimony is given under oath.

equity—a branch or system of jurisprudence in which one can obtain special relief. One who requests "equitable relief" must usually allege that he has "no adequate remedy at law," that is, he cannot expect to be fairly compensated by money damages, and needs other forms of relief such as an injunction.

escrow—a document or fund placed in the hand of another until the happening of some event. For example, your attorney may hold the settlement check in escrow until the other side receives all of the documents closing the case.

eviction—the act of dispossessing a tenant or other person in possession. Often accomplished by a "summary dispossess action." (See Chapter 2.)

ex parte—one side only. An ex parte application is made by one party to a lawsuit without notice to the other side.

ex post facto law—a law passed after the occurrence of the fact or event it makes illegal. A law enacted in 1980 stating that it was a crime for anyone to own or operate a motorcycle in 1970 would be an ex post facto law, and would be a violation of the Constitution.

extradition—the surrender by one state to another of a person accused of a crime. Usually, the governor of the state which wants to try the criminal must request extradition.

felony—a crime of serious nature (as opposed to a misdemeanor). Examples include murder, rape, and robbery.

fiduciary—a person who occupies a position of trust or responsibility, such as a trustee. Under the law, a fiduciary is held to a higher standard of conduct than an ordinary person.

fixture—an object or chattel attached permanently to a building or other structure.

franchise—the right granted by a franchisor to a franchisee to distribute the franchisor's service or product by operating his (the franchisee's) individually owned business as though it were part of the franchisor's large chain.

fraud—a false statement made with intent to deceive another person. Also referred to as "fraudulent misrepresentation."

garnishment—a process or proceeding whereby A's property or money in the hands of B is applied to payment of a debt owed to C, a creditor. Example: A has failed to pay money owed to C, and C wins a judgment in court allowing C to garnish money held in A's bank account at B bank.

gravamen—the crucial or material part of a charge or complaint.

habeas corpus—literally translated, "you have the body." A writ of habeas corpus is usually filed for the purpose of having a prisoner immediately brought before a court so that the court can determine if he or she is being held properly and in accord with due process.

hearsay—evidence given by a witness not from his personal knowledge, but from repetition of what he has heard others say. Hearsay evidence is not admissible in court. However, there are so many exceptions to this rule that it is probably more accurate to say that hearsay evidence is admissible if it falls within certain categories.

heir—a person who inherits property from one who dies without a will, although now also used to describe a person who inherits under the provisions of a will.

holographic will—a will written by the testator in his or her own hand.

impeach—in courtroom jargon, to dispute, contradict, or call into question the statements made by a witness. A witness whose credibility is impeached is usually not believed by a jury.

implead—to bring a third party into a lawsuit. Example: A sues B for injuries sustained in an automobile accident. B may implead C, claiming that C was really responsible for the accident.

injunction—an order issued by a court restraining or preventing one party from acting. A TRO is a temporary restraining order, or injunction, issued at the very outset of a case. Courts are usually reluctant to issue an injunction at these early stages and will do so only when the party requesting it can show that he or she will suffer "irreparable harm" unless it is issued.

interrogatories—a series of written questions prepared by one party to a lawsuit and which must be answered in writing by another party.

intestate—without making a will. If a person dies intestate, his property will be distributed to his heirs under the provisions of state law.

judgment—official decision by a court.

jurisdiction—the authority of a particular court to hear a case. A court will hear a case only if (1) personal jurisdiction has been obtained over the defendant and (2) the court has subject-matter jurisdiction—that is, the court is authorized by law to hear the type of case or to grant the type of relief requested by the parties.

jury—a panel of men and women selected to hear evidence. A petit jury is a jury empaneled to hear evidence in a civil and criminal trial and to render a verdict. At one time a petit jury was composed of twelve people, but now it is frequently composed of six. A grand jury (composed of a greater number of jurors than the petit jury) is empaneled to hear evidence of criminal activity and determine whether any individual should be indicted for these activities and brought to trial.

laches—undue delay or failure to press a legal claim.

lawyer—see *attorney*.

lease—an agreement to rent property for a period of time. Usually used in relation to an apartment or a portion of real property, but it can refer to an agreement to rent an automobile or machinery for a specific period of time. (See Chapter 2.)

legatee—a person who inherits property under the terms of a will.

libel—a false statement made in writing or pictures that humiliates or injures a person. A written statement, no matter how vicious, is not libelous if it is true.

license—authority or permission to do something, as in a license to conduct business.

lien—a claim on property to secure payment of a debt or obligation. If you take your automobile to a mechanic for repair, the mechanic may have a lien on your car for the value of his work.

malicious prosecution—an action begun with the intention of injuring the defendant and without proper cause.

merchantable—fair for the market, sound and without defect. When goods are sold by A to B there is an implied warranty of merchantability.

misdemeanor—a criminal act lower than a felony. A misdemeanor is usually punishable by a fine or short term in prison.

moot court—a special court session held for arguing moot cases or questions. Law schools schedule moot court sessions to help students gain experience.

motion—a procedure brought by an attorney to obtain a decision or ruling by a court on some point of law, usually prior to trial. An attorney may file a motion for a preliminary injunction or a motion to compel the other party to appear at a deposition.

negligence—failure to do something or to perform as a reasonable or prudent man would. "Contributory negligence" is a negligent act on the part of the complaining party which contributes to the injury.

nolo contendere—a plea of "no contest" by a defendant in a criminal case. It has the same legal effect as a guilty plea.

nominal damages—a small or trifling amount awarded to a party in a legal action. Usually awarded in cases where the party filing suit shows that he has been injured, or his rights have been violated, but cannot demonstrate that he has suffered a substantial loss for which he should be compensated.

novation—substitution of a new contract or agreement for an old one.

Noncupative Will—an oral will declared by a testator before witnesses. A noncupative will is not always valid.

parol—oral; not set down in writing.

per curiam—an opinion written by the entire court rather than an opinion by any one judge.

perjury—a false statement made under oath. Perjury is a criminal offense.

plaintiff—the one who initiates a lawsuit. Sometimes called the "petitioner" or "complainant."

pledge—a delivery of goods to a creditor as security for a debt. Legal title to the goods remains with the owner.

polling the jury—a practice whereby each individual juror is asked if he assents to the verdict announced by the foreman of the jury.

possession—"nine tenths of the law." "Adverse possession" is "open and notorious" possession of real property by one who is not the true owner for a certain length of time.

power of attorney—a written document authorizing another person to act as one's agent or attorney.

preponderance of the evidence—greater weight of the evidence or more convincing evidence. A jury in a civil case is usually asked to decide the case in favor of the party who has presented a preponderance of the credible evidence.

prima facie—from the Latin, meaning at first sight, or on the face of it. A person who sues establishes a "prima facie case" if he presents sufficient evidence to support his claim. The other party is then called on to produce contrary or rebuttal evidence.

probate—a judicial determination establishing the validity of a will. Also used to describe the procedure of having a will validated.

promissory note—a promise made in writing to pay a specified sum of money on demand or on a specified date.

proof beyond a reasonable doubt—proof which excludes any other reasonable hypothesis. A jury in a criminal case is told that it should vote to convict the defendant only if it finds that his guilt has been proved "beyond a reasonable doubt."

punitive damages—damages assessed by a court not to compensate a party for injuries suffered but to punish the other side for willful or malicious behavior. Sometimes referred to as "exemplary damages."

real property—land and any buildings erected on the land. All other property is usually classified under the heading "personal property."

referee—a person to whom a case is referred. The referee usually hears evidence and then submits his report or findings to the court.

release—a document discharging another party from all claims or actions which exist at the time. If A sues B for $5,000, and the two parties agree to settle the case for $3,000, B will ask A to provide him with a release when the $3,000 is paid.

replevin—a type of legal action brought to recover goods improperly taken.

reply—response to a counterclaim. A sues B. B then submits an answer and a counterclaim against A. A then submits a "reply" to the allegations made in the counterclaim.

res—a thing or object.

res judicata—the legal principle that a matter of controversy that is decided cannot be relitigated. A phrase used in civil practice. A sues B for breach of contract. A loses and fails to appeal the case. A cannot sue B again for the same breach of contract, since the matter is res judicata.

rescission—an action requesting the court to declare a contract or document null and void. A decision rescinding a contract means that the party is no longer bound by it.

retainer—fee for professional services charged by a lawyer. Now it is frequently used to describe only the initial fee paid by a client.

scienter—knowledge. The word is often used in legal papers to signify the defendant's guilty knowledge.

service of process—usually refers to service of legal papers on a defendant in a civil suit.

sewer service—false service of papers by a process server. Derives from the idea that an unethical process server would throw the legal papers in the sewer and then swear they were delivered to the defendant.

slander—speaking false and defamatory words (as distinguished from libel, which relates to the written word).

stare decisis—the policy of the courts to abide by and follow precedent.

statute of frauds—statutes which require certain classes of contracts to be in writing. The original statute was adopted in England and was entitled "An Act for the Prevention of Frauds and Perjuries." Now the individual states have adopted their own statutes.

statute of limitations—This term refers to a period of time in which a suit must be brought. Each state has adopted its own statute of limitations for various types of cases. In New York, for example, the statute of limitations for a libel action is one year.

stipulation—an agreement by the attorneys on opposite sides of a case, usually put in written form.

stockholder's derivative suit—a proceeding by a stockholder in his own name but really for the benefit of the corporation, usually alleging that the corporate officers or directors acted improperly.

subpoena—a document requiring a witness to appear and give testimony.

subpoena duces tecum—a document requiring a witness to appear with records or papers pertinent to the case.

summary judgment—a decision by a court (prior to trial) on the basis of the law, when there are no genuine facts in dispute.

surrogate—name used in some jurisdictions to describe the judge who administers probate matters, estates, etc.

testate—one who dies "testate" dies leaving a will. The one who makes the will is called a testator.

tort—a civil wrong. This is an area of the law that includes assault, false imprisonment, negligence, libel, and slander.

tort-feasor—one who commits a tort.

trademark—any word or symbol used by a manufacturer or merchant to identify or distinguish his goods from those manufactured or sold by others. (See Chapter 11.)

unjust enrichment—an equitable doctrine that provides that one should not be allowed to enrich himself unfairly at another's expense.

venue—the county or district where a legal action is brought. Under certain circumstances a party may request a "change of venue."

verdict—a decision or finding made by a jury. In a criminal trial, a jury can return with a verdict of "guilty" or "not guilty."

warranty—a promise, either expressed or implied, that goods are of a certain quality or fit for a particular purpose.

Index

Index